Business Development Turbo-Charged

Dr. Earl R. Smith II

Raven Press

Copyright 2014 Dr. Earl R. Smith II

Acknowledgements

Every author owes a debt of gratitude to the people who have influenced their lives and helped them gain the knowledge and experience which allows them to write something meaningful. This is truer with this author and book than most. None of it would be possible without the friendship and support of a wide range of people – some remain close friends while others were good Samaritans that I met along the way. Their wisdom and kindnesses have helped me to find my way through a bedeviling maze to enlightenment. Such gifts are priceless and I am forever grateful for them.

Most of my early companies were focused on designing and producing investment opportunities for major clients of what was then called the 'big eight' accounting firms and the front line Wall Street investment banking houses. The legions of people within both sets of organizations that supported me have a special place in memory. They trusted me with their most valuable assets – the very core of their business. Without them I could not have enjoyed the success that I have.

Among all these people, I want to single out David Moxley – one of the last true managing partners of Touche Ross – when there was such an organization. His kindness and mentoring made a huge difference in my life. I learned a great deal from Dave – not just about business but about the nature and texture of humanity.

Along the way I have had the great fortune of associating with dozens of CEOs and other senior executives. I have constantly been blessed by their willingness to share their experiences and to engage in open and highly productive discussions. In truth, thinking without doing has little effect in business and the doing of one life is not enough to build an understanding of a complex and subtle process like getting business development right. Without their friendship and mentoring this book would not have been possible.

Many senior executives have given me an opportunity to help them and their company through senior advisory, board membership and other roles. I have always seen this willingness as the highest compliment that any executive can give – to allow a stranger into the inner sanctum and trust their intentions. Strong personal relationships have almost always grown out of these experiences – we have fought the wars and mostly won – and mostly is better than most!

Finally, I have had the opportunity to write articles for a number of print and internet publications. I am grateful to the publishers and editors for giving my voice a chance to be heard.

The response to these writings has always been an important reward. Many readers have taken the time to constructively respond to my articles. Others have shared their 'war stories'. For any writer, a reader's response is always a rewarding experience – an indication that all the thinking and work has reached another and proven valuable. For me, these rewards have been particularly sweet. I have never written a word that I did not get three to four in return. A two thousand word article generally brought six to eight thousand words in response. For that experience I feel particularly blessed. I want to thank every one of those kind and considerate people who took the time and made the effort to respond

About Dr. Smith

I provide mentoring to those who have both the courage and determination to make a truly transformational journey. My approach is heavily influenced by core principles of Zen Buddhism. I don't offer quick fixes or follow the latest fads. If you are willing to make the long journey – if it's time for you to come to know the person you really are and can become – if you intend to finally find the path you should be following – if you want to start living life you were truly meant to live – then perhaps we should talk. Send me an e-mail and we'll arrange a time to chat. DrSmith@Dr-Smith.com.

Other Books by Dr. Smith

Zen Mentoring – Forty Meditations
The CEO's Handbook Volume One - 46 Meditations for the Thinking Chief Executive
The CEO's Handbook Volume Two - Business Development the Right Way
The CEO's Handbook Volume Three - The Money Chase: Angle Investors and Venture Capitalists
The CEO's Handbook Volume Four – Getting Funded by Angle Investors
The CEO's Handbook Volume Four – Venture Funding
Understanding Venture Capital
Mentoring Leadership
Dream Walk - Parables for the Living
Twitter Super-Charged

About Ian MacGregger and the Omega/Alpha Series

Ian MacGregger is Anna's confidential assistant. She's a paranormal private detective with an amazing range of skills and abilities. A genius to be sure but a great deal more. Now, with Anna's permission, he writes about some of their more interesting cases.

Books by Ian MacGregger

The Cabal - Volume One: The Toast of Broadway: What begins as a series of bizarre murders in the theater district of Manhattan quickly develops into a global struggle against an international criminal cabal.

The Cabal - Volume Two: Marked For Murder: After solving the Broadway murders case and, in the process, dealing a heavy blow to the Cabal, the enemy decides to strike back. They marshal all there resources to punish Anna and her family. The Cabal has marked them all for murder.

The Cabal – Volume Three: The Sound of Fury: The tranquility at Omega is shattered by the assassination of an honored visitor. The killing is just a prelude to a series of horrific attacks. The leader of the Cabal shows herself to be a far more formidable adversary than Anna has ever faced before.

Table of Contents

Introduction 7

The Conundrum that is Business Development

Chapter 1: Five Reasons Why Business Development Is So Difficult To Get Right 12
Chapter 2: Seven Reasons Why Advisory Boards Don't Produce 15
Chapter 3: Battle at the Cottage Gate 22
Chapter 4: Dysfunctional Advisory Boards – A Family of Problems 28
Chapter 5: Advisory Boards as Business Development Engines – The Beginnings 32

Advisory Boards

Chapter 1: Turbocharged Business Development 35
Chapter 2: Benefits and Costs 43
Chapter 3: John's Questions – Round Two 52
Chapter 4: Change Management 61

Planning for Two Journeys

Chapter 1: Change Management 71
Chapter 2: Board Design and Population 79

A Working Board

Chapter 1: The First Board Meeting 86
Chapter 2: Conflict, Renegotiation and Removal 97
Chapter 3: First Blood 102

On Leadership 107

Chapter 1: Leadership That Empowers – The Fire of the Mind 108
Chapter 2: Leadership that Limits - The 'Completeness Doctrine' 112
Chapter 3: A Balanced Senior Management Team 116

Managing Mt. Rushmore 122

Retrospective

Chapter 1: Anniversary 133
Chapter 2: Assessing the Impact 137

Final Thoughts 139

Contact Information 141

Introduction

Why does business development never seem to fully live up to its name?

Why is it so difficult to get business development working effectively for your company?

Why does your BD team look like a series of revolving doors - with one person after another being hired amid great fanfare only to be let go within a year for 'non-performance'?

All these consultants are peddling the same tired old solutions to a problem that never seems to go away. Why can't somebody come up with something that works?

There has to be a better way!

The Good News

I've never met a CEO who was really happy with the way business development was working. They all end up saying about the same thing. *"Traditional solutions fail to produce expected results while regularly generating unexpected costs. There needs to be a better way."*

"Why can't we get this right? It's not rocket science and we're supposed to be good at what we do. Why can't we get this damn thing right?" I remember the look of utter frustration. I had started three companies by then and knew exactly what this CEO was talking about. Business development is the major challenge of every CEO and senior team.

Being in business begins with getting business. Get it right and you can win big. Get it wrong and nothing else much matters. For all my experience, I had little to suggest to my frustrated companion – it was very humbling. After we parted, my walk up First Avenue towards my home on 59th Street in Manhattan became the first steps on a decade's long quest for a solution.

During my six tours as CEO I have encountered the same challenges over and over. My frustration grew until there was no way out but to find an alternative approach that really worked.

Finding a way to make business development work became a crusade.

I got very lucky. My fourth company showed me the way. Six months after my dismal performance in the bar I had the beginnings of a solution. Those first insights formed the core of an innovative, potent and cost-effective approach to business development.

Much of the next two decades were been spent developing then refining a solution to what I see as <u>the</u> principal point of pain for most CEOs. During that time I was guided by three goals.

- First, the solution had to be head-and-shoulders better than competing strategies.
- Second, it had to be highly cost effective – minimizing the drain on critical resources while generating maximum benefits in the form of turbo-charged business development.
- And third, it had to work!

So, here is the good news – there <u>is</u> a better way and this book is going to show you how to turn all those nagging questions into fading memories.

Business Development Turbo-Charged describes how an advisory board populated with highly experienced, committed and well-connected individuals is the fastest and most effective way to drive a company's top line. This book describes the design, operation and management of such boards – boards that will radically increase the effectiveness of a company's business development process.

Business Development Turbo-Charged shows you how it is done and, more importantly, that it can be done for virtually any company with amazing results. Its core messages are that:

1. Getting business development right is <u>the</u> primary challenge for any senior team,
2. There is a solution to this persistent and painful challenge;

3. The solution is potent and cost effective and,
4. Given a professional approach, this solution is not rocket science – it can be deployed for virtually any company.

In this book you will read about the design, population and management of these boards and how they can radically increase the effectiveness of a company's business development process.

Why This Book Is Important

Every senior executive's future, no matter what their title, depends on how well business development works. Your own future depends on how well it is managed within your company. Many CEOs and other senior executives have become addicted to courses and seminars on the subject. They move from one guru to another only to be disappointed yet again. All they seem to be accomplishing is moving the flatware around on the table – nothing fundamental seems to change and the food never shows up. The cycle goes on and on – with precious time and resources being wasted. So why is this happening?

The basic reason is that none of the offered solutions adequately address the fundamental issues – that the science and art of business development as it is traditionally practiced is inadequate to the challenges that companies now face. *Business Development Turbo-Charged* provides you with an entirely new approach. This book will help you break that cycle and set off on a new, highly productive path. It can help you meet a challenge that affects your future and the future of your company – and <u>that</u> makes it very important.

Mentoring As a Bonus

"Once we launched the board, I realized that none of my senior team had ever had a true mentor. I realized that I had never had one either. Now we all have very experienced people working with us – helping us to perfect our craft. That alone is worth the price of the board – the increased business is almost just a bonus"

That was one CEO's comment on the impact of an advisory board. Modern corporate culture does not foster mentoring relationships as effectively as traditional ones did. With boards these mentoring relationships naturally develop. CEOs and senior team members now realize that they are not in it alone – that there are very experienced people that they can trust and who will provide advice and guidance where it has been lacking in the past. In many cases these mentoring relationships are life changing.

Structure of the Book

There are two kinds of chapters. The first describes a fictionalized set of meetings with the CEO (John Slate) and senior team of a fictional company (Rocket Science). For these chapters, I have drawn from dozens of client relationships and have tried to give you a sense of 'actually being there'. Although Rocket Science and its senior team are <u>purely fictional</u>, they represent accurately the process, responses, challenges, successes, failures and results that actual clients have experienced.

Other chapters focus on important concepts. I have included chapters on some of the core concepts, change management, board design and population, leadership and the management of the boards. All of these are designed to help you reach a deeper understanding of the boards and what is required to make them work well.

I suggest particular attention to the section on leadership. The first challenge to any CEO who embarks on such a path is their ability to grow – to reinvent themselves to meet the needs of their evolving company. I have focused on two areas – empowering leadership and limiting leadership. There is also a chapter on the developing a balanced senior team. This idea is so core to the process of setting up an advisory board to drive the run-rate, that it probably should have more attention than I can give it in this volume.

As you will read over and over, the process of designing, populating, standing up and managing an advisory board as a business development engine is complex. It requires subtlety and a sophisticated and knowledgeable approach. I have tried to highlight important concepts and give you a sense of why they are important and how they impact the prospects of any company and its board.

Material for the book has been drawn from personal experiences with dozens of C-level executives, consultants and members of boards of directors and advisory boards. The goal of the book is to help you understand the value proposition behind advisory boards as business development engines and that this new approach to an old problem is the most effective way to make business development live up to its name. Be prepared to be amazed! It is truly *Business Development Turbo-Charged.*

Washington, DC
July 2014

The Conundrum that is Business Development

Chapter 1: Five Reasons Why Business Development Is So Difficult To Get Right

Every conversation I have with a CEO eventually touches on the same conundrum - '*How in the world does a company get traction in new markets with new clients?*' This challenge seems to rank right up there with arranging adequate financial resources and getting top people to join the team.

This challenge often did not limit growth in the early stages. During that time, the contacts and reputation of the founders and key executives drove the 'top line'. Most often the client base came to resemble a silo in a corn field - one client dominating the business mix surrounded by other smaller ones that represented stunted attempts at broadening the base.

To be sure, this start up strategy is one of the preferred ways forward during a company or division's early stages. In fact it is an early indicator that the management team has any business starting the business at all. If they don't have ready clients for their product of service, they should get them before going forward.

But why, once the early growth phase is over, is it so difficult to keep business development going? Why do the business development slots look so much like revolving doors? And, why is it that growing a company from nil to ten or fifteen million in annual revenues often does not seem to prepare management to take it to thirty or fifty million?

Reason One: The senior management (particularly the CEO) is not really committed to making the journey. This is more common than you might think. Corporate growth requires significant self-reinvention among key members of the senior team. Often they are not prepared to give up control or manage a larger operation. Some prefer 'writing code' or whatever the company's principal business happens to be. But whatever their 'rationale', they don't want to or can't become managers. In this case, expenditures on business development can just be a waste of resources. Better save the money and buy the new car.

Reason Two: The structure pretty much guarantees failure. Business development is often an afterthought add-on to the evolved organizational structure. It seems to operate in a quasi-independent status with loose reporting arrangements to the CEO or COO. It is an appendage after the fact. Business development has to be integral to the company's organizational structure and the CEO needs to be the senior business development member of the team.

I once attended an all-hands retreat of a company where the COO gave the business development report. That spoke volumes on how the company saw the three business development employees standing in the wings. They were, of course, replaced by newer models by the next retreat and the revolving door was kept in good working order.

Reason Three: Business development is seen as the province of middle-level people. Think of the message that such an approach gives potential new clients. *"Talk to the 'lessers' and, if we deem you worthy, we will let you talk to the senior people."* New clients need/want to see the top person right off the get-go. It is the CEO that represents the company's commitment to client satisfaction, the ability of the company to commit as well as the ability of the client to find some person to rely on. Each time a decision-maker chooses to go with a new company they take a huge risk. If it goes wrong - how much faith do you think such a person would put in a middle level person with no real connection to the company's culture or senior management team?

Reason Four: The wrong people for the job: A company often will bring in 'business development' types as a first attempt to attack the problem of widening the client base. These people are 'specialists' in chasing business - but frequently not specialists in the business of the company. Most often they are walled-off from the company's principal clients and are limited to higher risk, longer cycle targets. What is most interesting about this approach is that it resource-starves functions that a company needs to provide in order to successfully grow its top line. Money is spent on business development types while the proposal development, capture and red-teaming are radically under-resourced. In the end it is often the case of a middle level employee identifying a marginal piece of business that the company cannot properly pursue and capture.

Reason Five: What is all this making us look like in the market place? The process is called <u>branding</u> - establishing the reputation of the company in the minds of actual and potential customers. It is by far the least understood and most dangerous threat to any company's future. How is your company known - what is its reputation? How well do you understand why customers do business with you? Are you known as a group that knows how business is done? Or are you branded as a company that has 'out-sourced' its future? These 'costs' are often overlooked as being less important than the business of the business. This mistake has probably killed more companies than any other. How you are known determines how seriously you are taken - and that largely determines what opportunities you will see and how successful you will become.

There are more reasons than these five but I suspect that you are getting the idea. Business development is a tough nut to crack for any management team intent on growing it company. There are more dead bodies in that field than live travelers. Without careful planning and disciplined execution, the results are likely to be both disappointing and frustrating.

Chapter 2: Seven Reasons Why Advisory Boards Don't Produce

My company builds and manages advisory boards as business development engines for emerging and well-established companies. Properly designed and managed, they are the single most powerful component of business development that I have ever found – bar none! The process of setting up and managing the boards is one of the most fulfilling roles that I play.

I am often the first contact with CEOs who have become frustrated with the lack of effectiveness of their business development strategies and have decided to seek out another way. They might have read one of my articles on my advisory boards and contacted me to see if our approach could make a difference with their company. Others are referred by friends who are trying to help. It is often the first step in a journey that changes forever the way the CEO looks at the process of business development and their role in it.

Many of these companies already have advisory boards that haven't been productive. Dissatisfaction with the lack of results is often a primary driver. CEOs are frustrated by unfulfilled promises and are determined to find a better way. These conversations, and the engagements that have followed, have yielded a pile of war stories. Patterns have emerged. Here are seven of the most common reasons that advisory boards fail to produce significant value:

The Logical Imperative: Advisory boards get formed for all sorts of reasons - most of them ineffectual and some flatly unwise. In most cases boards seemed to have been formed under what I call the 'logical imperative'.

"Of course we'll have an advisory board! Let's pull one together just like those guys did. Of course it will focus on advising us on technology issues – or management issues. It will be a coffee clutch – a collegiate meeting of like minds. We'll meet once a month – or (somewhat later) once a quarter. It will be great!"

Well, maybe you get the picture. The point is that the founders have not carefully thought through why they are forming the board. For the most part they have not even thought through a proper mission. Most have no real experience with a highly productive board and end up doing what seems like the logical thing to do at the time. It all seems so intuitive that the board seems to form itself. Many times it is a 'peer-gathering' group - *"I'll be on your board and you on mine."* These boards are almost always net-zero undertakings at best and net-negative in the long run. Logical imperatives tend to lead to ineffectual gaggles rather than productive, working boards.

Dangerous Liaisons: For some reason lots of CEOs never seem to put the words 'corporate' and 'espionage' together. They build advisory boards (I suspect out of a suspicion of personal or professional inadequacy) to advise them on technology and/or management issues. Over and over I come across boards that regularly see the latest and neatest advances of a company – boards that are populated with people who have interests outside their board participation. *"Oh, no – I trust these people,"* I am often told. These statements remind me of a story about a young woman who was visiting her spinster aunt. While they were having tea in the parlor a cat wandered in with a litter of new kittens.

"Oh, aren't they so cute," said the visitor.

"Yes they are – but I can't figure out how they happened. Fluffy is a house cat and she never goes outside.

As she was talking a clearly virile tom cat came into the room and stretched sensuously. *"What about him,"* inquired the girl?"

"Oh no, couldn't be Tom," said the aunt. *"He's her brother!"*

I'll leave you to follow the story where it leads – but the point should be clear enough. Too late smart is, first and foremost, too late.

Who's Minding the Store: Often when reviewing the history and mission of ineffectual boards I find that there has been no clear mission for the board, no defined strategy for managing the board and no formal metrics for measuring effectiveness and performance. The CEO is nominally in charge but the board is managed only during the times just preceding, during and following meetings. For the rest of the time it is mostly ignored with little contact between board members and the senior team.

Additionally, the lack of clear, effective and enforced metrics has defined a culture that virtually guarantees little or no production. Many times board members serve based on a 'verbal agreement' – and, as the saying goes. *"a verbal agreement isn't worth the paper it's written on!"*

When it comes to such a board, you see leadership without purposefulness and participation without responsibility. Meetings tend to be rambling discussions on management style, Monday morning quarterbacking the CEO and water cooler type hashing and re-hashing of corporate gossip. Board members, who see a leadership without apparent purpose or concern with purpose, react similarly. Over time these boards tend to discuss the same issues over and over again until the members get bored and the merry-go-round slows down and finally stops.

What Mission Statement: *"What's it good for? Absolutely nothing!"* Logical imperatives, dangerous liaisons and inattentive management lead to just that. Wasted energy, lost opportunities and negative branding are the most common result of this combination. Yes, negative branding! I have dismantled boards and interviewed lots of 'advisors' – some of whom have spent many frustrating years on ineffectual boards. Often I was sure that the ears of the senior corporate team had to be burning. And these are supposed to be their friends!

Oh, you think that your advisors always say such good things about you? Well, wake up and smell the decaying flesh! If you are wasting their time and the company's resources, if you are risking their reputation, if you are acting more like a den mother than a CEO, if your ego seems to be the most important part of your anatomy – what do you think they are going to say? A board should, from its very conception, have a clear mission statement. Board members should be recruited with that mission statement front-and-center. They should clearly understand what will be expected of them, how they will be paid and what will happen if expectations are not met. Without this, forget the idea of having a board – it will just become a kamikaze raid on a vacant lot!

Wisdom on the Cheap: There is a whole category out there – thieves parading as CEOs and senior team members. Visit any chat room dedicated to start-ups and you can listen in on the same conversation over and over. Most of them start with the premise that it is unwise to pay advisors in any but an incentivized way – in other words only based on the results they generate. Although incentivized compensation is an important component of any good advisory agreement, there needs to be a base of recognition for service.

But these people take the argument to the extreme. In one recent thread a series of so-called CEOs weighed in with almost identical observations. Most of them had war stories about consultants that had taken their money and produced very little. As the single-perspective discussion reached its peak, I introduced two ideas into the mix. First, aren't selections of non-productive consultants a direct reflection on the 'decider' and the inadequacies of the process of selection and engagement? And second, if you limit the pool of possible consultants to those who will work only for incentivized compensation, don't you filter out professionals whose track record of production puts them in a position to require non-incentivized compensation?

You would think that I had dropped a cat into a box full of mice! *"Oh no, it wasn't me ... it was 'them'."* The so-called CEOs all considered it a failure on the part of the consultant. 'Blame the other' was the theme! Psychologists have a term for this kind of denial of responsibility. Look, you either believe that there are people out there who have knowledge and connections that can help you or you don't. If you do, you go out and find them then make agreements which reflect the reality of the market for their services. The onus is on you to search effectively and reach productive agreements – even if it taxes your company's resources.

Any expenditure must yield a return on investment and any agreement must specify performance metrics – but no professional would find that onerous. My experience is that no well-connected person, with a serious intent and ability to make a contribution, will give away that potential in exchange for a purely conditional compensation. In other words, you get what you pay for!

CEOs who can successfully navigate these waters have a substantial leg up on their competitors. It is a skill that needs to be learned both to avoid the waste of non-productive relationships and to reap the benefits of productive ones. Wisdom on the cheap is just another tilt at yet another windmill.

Making Love to the Inertia: Many of my engagements begin with the dismantling of an existing advisory board. Most of these boards were formed amid much enthusiasm – with members happy to have a chance to contribute. But over time, and with a declining enthusiasm, they have simply ceased to function. For the most part little of this is the fault of the board members. They are, after all, not officers of the company and have been asked to help it succeed by people who they expected to help them do just that. But inertia is overwhelming in the face of the lack of intent – and intent is driven by leadership. Management often falls in love with the inertia that these boards allow and that is a recipe for disaster.

My suspicion is that, in the face of a wildly chaotic world, they see the board as a kind of oasis – a quiet place to go to have peaceful conversations with fellow travelers. Without connection to the imperatives that are driving the rest of the company, these boards languish into unproductively neutral cultures. Finally they ossify into a mass of inertia. The end has arrived – it doesn't matter how much longer the board is in existence. It becomes the proverbial 'dead man walking'. Execution is often the merciful thing.

We're Ready for Prime Time - Not: I get this one a lot! A CEO reads some of my stuff and comes to the conclusion that *"I've just got to have one of those boards."* So we have our initial meeting. I talk a lot about how the company has to ready itself for a board. The middle-level business development types will become a liability and need to be replaced with far more experienced team members. The resourcing of targeting, proposal development, red-team and capture will have to be beefed up if the company is going to take advantage of the opportunities that an advisory board can make available. There is a lot to be done in getting ready.

I emphasize that this is a complex process that has to be approached professionally and with careful preparation. Then it comes. *"I don't think that we need all this 'getting ready'. Why don't you just go out and get me some advisors?"* At first I am patient and explain that very important people will not be willing to risk their reputations with a company ill prepared to take advantage of their assistance. Then I get something like:

"This is obvious and it should be a concern of yours. However, not in our case. We do have considerable experience working with 'very senior and highly professional' people and also, we are quite capable of executing."

This is virtually a direct quote from a CEO whose advisory board had been completely unproductive and whose company was about to run out of resources because of management's complete failure to generate significant volumes of business! The hard truth is that the advisors that I place on my boards care deeply about preserving and extending their reputations. They are not about to risk them on such representations. They know a whole lot better than that! You should as well. This mutual understanding is the gateway to a more productive way of relating to the process of business development for your company.

They Can Work – and Work Beyond Your Wildest Dreams: The single most amazing thing about these discussions is that, despite all of the hazards and misunderstandings, many of them lead to productive engagements that produce results. Perhaps one out of three CEOs get through the kinds of challenges outlined above. And, out of those, somewhere around four in ten actually begin the process of forming a board.

In an important way the process is self-selecting. CEOs who can understand and adapt to a new approach to business development are precisely the right candidates for having, and learning to benefit from, an advisory board. It is these four-in-thirty that make the entire process such a joy for me and the professionals I associate with. For, once the preliminaries are out of the way, the real magic begins. The old saw is that 'nothing succeeds like success.' Well nothing feels better than helping someone succeed beyond their wildest dreams.

Chapter 3: Battle at the Cottage Gate

I sometimes work with companies that are on the verge of leaving the 'cottage stage' and pushing into the great uncertainty of corporate adolescence. This push, and the stress which often accompanies it, is one of the seminal periods in the development of any company. By the time I arrive on the scene, battle lines often have been well formed and the organization has divided into two camps. The coming battle will present severe challenges for the founders, senior team and the company. The prevailing camp will get to decide what the future will hold for all involved.

Let me start by defining what I mean by 'cottage stage'. First off, defining a company in terms of its gross revenue is not useful. I've seen organizations generating close to thirty million dollars in gross revenue while still operating within this paradigm. Secondly, the size of the organization in terms of its client base or human resources is also not a good indicator. I have encountered companies with twenty to thirty major clients and over a hundred employees that are still operating as a cottage business. Finally, the age of a company is an unreliable indicator as well. Once a company slips into what I call 'life-style mode' it enters a period of repressed adolescence that can last through its entire life span.

There are a number of indicators which are very useful in identifying a company which is still operating within the 'cottage' paradigm and facing the complex issues of reinventing itself. The most notable of them are: the evolving nature of leadership, the changing nature of employees, the definition of span of control, the performance and behavior of the founders, the level of professionalism within the corporate culture and the ability of the company to allow its culture to evolve in order to cope with the increasing burdens that always accompany rapid growth and increased size.

The Evolving Nature of leadership: In the cottage stage, leadership tends to be defined by the founders. For many, because of their own rather limited management experience, the dominate vision of leadership tends to be based on position and prerogative rather than inspiration and example. This can work during the early stages.

But, as the company grows, it comes under increasing pressure to bring in more experienced managers. These newcomers tend to pose an immediate threat to the prevailing theory of leadership. In a sense a new coin of the realm begins to circulate and compete with the old currency. Employees now face a choice that wasn't available earlier on. On the one hand there are the founders who may continue to insist that they are the leaders and should be followed - often without question. On the other there are managers bringing new, and often very creative, approaches. Their leadership is based on the proposition of 'do as I do' rather than 'do as I say' - and they lead by example.

Founders are often the ones most challenged by this evolution in the operative concept of leadership. It takes an exceptional person to give up the security of the '*I own the business so you will do as I say*' attitude in favor of the more risky and challenging '*follow me when I need to lead and I will follow you when it is better that you lead*'. How the founders react to this option has a major impact on the future of the company.

The Changing Nature of Employees: As an organization grows, and the pressures to generate higher performance increase, employees will seek out leadership and form allegiances which will empower them to meet new, and far more difficult, challenges. New managers may have experience and skill sets that were not present in the original team. Some of them will take leadership roles in areas that have traditionally been the prerogative of the founders - resulting in tensions that are felt company-wide.

Over time, two camps evolve within the company. The first, which I call 'the traditionalists', tends to find these changes unsettling. They often wistfully reminisce about the 'good old days' when the company was more like a family than a business. They are bound together by a network of relationships, some of which are deeply personal. Their approach to the business tends to be conservative and focused on 'growing without major changes in the corporate culture'. As the battle approaches they will often adopt a Fort Apache the Bronx approach - circling the wagons and defending what they consider to be the pure heart and soul of the company.

On the other side of this developing divide is the new breed of employee whose vision of the company generally extends farther into the future. Their vision involves not only substantial continued growth but an increasingly professionalized environment which includes a professionalization of the management team - a significant and sustained evolution of the corporate culture. These employees tend to lack the emotional connection to the early stages of a company's growth. They've signed on not because they are true believers in the founders but were attracted to the opportunities that the company has now become able to offer.

The Definition of Span of Control: One of the early indicators of the coming battle is a widening disagreement over the concept of span of control. In traditional, modernist management terms span of control is defined in terms of a list of those individuals who report directly to a given person. This 'post-Fordist' vision is the most common one adopted by founders because, in the early stages, all roads lead to them. But this vision of an organization is fundamentally flawed.

In truth this rather basic version only works in the most primitive of organizational structures - when leadership is based upon prerogative and position. But things get considerably more complicated as the company's operations expand. Informal reporting patterns begin to evolve based upon perceived competence and charisma rather than prerogative and position.

Inevitably informal networks develop. Employees develop strong relationships with individuals they trust and respect and who relate to them in a supportive and empowering way. Pressures build when there is an increasing divergence between these informal and formal relationships.

The Performance and Behavior of the Founders: In the early stages of a company's growth most founders tend to fancy themselves as 'chief-of-everything'. They have 'final say' on virtually everything that affects the company. Few things are minor enough to escape their attention. But as the company grows this becomes practically impossible. (Although I have known several founders who have given the impossible a heroic and generally destructive shot.)

In purely human terms there becomes too much to understand and process – too many skills to master – too many places and people to be – for the founders to remain master of everything. Additionally, the challenges that a company faces as it grows become both more complex and specialized. Solutions require extensive knowledge and experience in skill areas – skill sets that the founders often do not have.

If the founders try to maintain their control, the company will be limited in its growth to the size that that management approach allows. It will grow until the internal pressures threaten to cause an implosion. Most often, founders who cannot bring themselves to let go and delegate will (sometimes unconsciously) work to keep the company a 'manageable size'. But if the founders successfully reinvent themselves, the team will expand to include new members with more sophisticated knowledge in important areas – people who will take the lead.

The Level of Professionalism within the Corporate Culture: When founders start out to build a company, there are many areas where they are just 'making it up as they go along'. Many of these are in the 'non-technology' parts of the business of growing a business. Finances can be managed out of the proverbial cigar box. HR is handled by visits to job boards or word-of-mouth searches. Decisions about which business opportunities to pursue are generally made opportunistically and with an eye towards survival. Little attention tends to be paid to the definition and evolution of a corporate culture – and the attention that is paid tends to be superficial.

There is some point in the evolution of every company that marks the beginning of the end of the viability of these kinds of 'off-the-cuff' strategies. They just don't seem to be working like the used to. Things get more complex and the need to have systems that are robust and effective increases. Also, the impact of failure tends to increase and the founders can spend more and more time crisis managing.

Professionalization of the team means bringing in new members who have deeper knowledge and experience in the process of running a company (and often less in the technology, product or service that is the company's foundation). Some major areas of professionalization that can cause internal stress are: proposal development and delivery, capture, red-teaming, sales, HR, financial control and general management. That these new skill sets are critical to the growth of any company is not the question. How a company deals with meeting or avoiding these needs is.

The Ability of the Company to Allow Its Culture to Evolve: An adult will do poorly in most civilized societies if they have repressed the process of maturing and are still acting like a child. The same is true of a company and its culture. Growth means change - but it also means evolution along well defined pathways.

There are often two broad paths that present themselves to a company moving out of the cottage stage and into adolescence. One road takes it towards what I call a 'life-style' company – one which meets primarily the needs of the founders leaving the rest of the team to decide whether their needs are being fulfilled. Along this road, employees have to accommodate the circumstances desired by the founders or leave in search of greener pastures – and many of the best often do.

The second road opens towards growth beyond expectations and focuses on meeting the needs of an expanding team. This option requires the founders to evolve in ways that allow them to help the team members meet their needs.

Corporate culture must evolve and become more adult-like if a company's growth is going to be sustainable. The issue becomes whether it is going to have the chance to grow and realize its potential. The founders are most often the gatekeepers.

The Ten Percenters: So how does a company decide between the paths of repressed adolescence on the one hand and maturing on the other? You probably noticed that I have made extensive references to the role and impact of the attitudes and capacities of the founders - so it will come as no surprise that I believe, at least initially, that the future is in their hands. The truth is that the founders make the first choices – choosing a path for their creation. These choices are often best if they are decisions to allow others to participate. Even so, these first steps are only the initial skirmishes in the battle.

I have seen battles at the cottage gates rage on for years - with both sides struggling for supremacy - while massive amounts of damage accrued. I have watched founders, in reaction to perceived challenges to their supremacy, resort to the nuclear option – become true dictators in their own house. In those cases the results have always been disastrous.

At other times one or more of them accomplish an evolutionary leap – reinventing themselves to a new type of leader and putting the status of founder on the shelf. Here progress is made and, over time, the battle may get resolved productively.

On more than one occasion I have seen the newer, more professional team members get fed up and go off on their own – leaving the cottage to the traditionalists. That result puts the company back to square one in the process and the battle lines tend to reform around the gate.

These battles rage on as long as issues such as the ones described above are potent and until one or the other side totally abandons the field. Two roads diverge in a leafy wood and the company can only take one. One leads to limits and eternal adolescence until death - the other to a path to healthy adulthood. The future is in the hands of the founders and the outlook is not rosy. My experience has been that, by their actions, rather than their words, seven out of ten founders drive their company towards the first path.

Chapter 4: Dysfunctional Advisory Boards – A Family of Problems

A well designed, populated and managed advisory board can bring substantial benefits. This is particularly true when it comes to the process of business development. Such a board can help senior management succeed beyond their wildest dreams. But there are reefs and shoals that need to be avoided.

Often a new client will have an existing advisory board. One of my early tasks in such situations is to *'fix it'*. At least that's how the CEO tends to put it. Most of these boards have common characteristics and most are indicators that the board needs to be dismantled and replaced.

The primary negative indicator is almost always a lack of productivity. Many have been in existence for years but have yet to directly make significant contributions. A secondary indicator is unproductive board meetings, which may have started out monthly but now, occur less and less frequently. Members have either lost enthusiasm or patience and become observers rather than players. Meetings tend to occur, if at all, without much prior preparation and with little, if any, structured agenda. The culture seems to be focused on maintaining camaraderie rather than high value creation. As a friend of mine used to say "*the wrong is over but the malady lingers on.*"

Some boards have become completely virtual. These represent a major effort in duel negative branding by senior management. They are indicative both of a failure in management and of a corporate culture of waste and inattention. Board members tend to fall into the 'rent-a-name' category. Not only do these boards typically have to be dismantled but a campaign needs to be mounted to overcome the accumulated damage to the corporate image - particularly within its client base. Doing it poorly is most often worse than not doing it at all.

Many of these boards include members who have been serving for years. Little if any tracking of their contributions to the company's growth has been done. In fact, there is often a total lack of metrics which defines effective board service.

The development of appropriate advisory board metrics is elementary school math. So the real question is, *"why do many companies with advisory boards not have appropriate metrics in place?"* I would suggest that the answer lies in a) how unseriously management takes the existence, value and potential contributions of the board and b) how poorly they intend to take advantage of the opportunities it could create. Of course, such a board will probably, if pressed, prove incapable of delivering solid value anyway.

At a strategic level, the purpose and charge of the board tends to be very poorly drawn. There is often no coherent document which describes either the function of the board or the manner in which performance will be measured. Matriculation to board membership tends to be casual. Given this, how effective would you suppose a board will be? How can everybody be on the same page when there is no page?

I see only one appropriate mission for an advisory board - driving the company's top line. A board should be populated by individuals who can help management identify, pursue and capture large pieces of business that they would not be able to without the board's assistance. As a result of this focus, board membership should be predicated on the ability of each member to contribute significantly to the company's growth. Individuals need to be able to open doors, influence decision-makers and help management organize a highly professional approach to capturing significant new business.

Once this focus is accepted, the evolution of metrics for effective board membership and advisory board performance becomes easy. Additionally the relationship between the board and management - particularly the relationship between the board and the CEO - becomes easy to define.

The compensation scheme for advisory board members is also fairly easy to draw. First there should be an annual retainer - a modest sum in recognition of board service. Second there should be a small honorarium for meeting participation and a provision for covering expenses. Most importantly, there should be an incentivized compensation agreement which is calculated based on the volume and quality of business brought in. Finally there should be a provision for achieving equity ownership after certain conditions, particularly conditions that relate to performance, have been met.

There is one characteristic of highly productive advisory boards that I've noticed over the years. And this one is going to stick in the craw of the CEOs who see themselves as 'chief of everything'. The best advisory boards are built by people from outside of the company for the company - by people who specialize in board design, population and management. Home grown boards tend to be underachievers. I think this is the case for two basic reasons. First, CEOs tend to prefer known people that they are comfortable with to people who will challenge them. Such 'comfortable' relationships will actually limit a board's productivity. Second, the CEO's connections tend to be at levels lower than is needed to populate an effective board.

The first of these can lead to boards that have collegiate but unproductive meetings. They tend towards feel-good societies which massage management's combined egos at the expense of shareholder value. Every board that I have built generates, particularly in its initial meetings, a strong sense of vertigo among senior management. Individual board members, often towards the end of long and highly successful careers, challenge management to get their collective acts together and the company in shape to deal with the increased business that the board can produce.

The second tendency can be more lethal than the first. Board members need to be very senior individuals with a wide range of contacts, current credibility in critical areas and a willingness to actually work through the entire process of identifying, chasing and capturing new business as an active and aggressive advocate for the company. Individual board members who do not meet these basic criteria will prove unproductive, and sometimes destructive, of board operations. 'Rent-a-Name' boards are most often pure overhead ... it is advocacy not introductions that is needed ... working partners rather than patrician purveyors of holy water. A critical characteristic of the individual who builds a board is that they have a very wide range of senior contacts and can manage a widely ranging search for effective members.

The design, population and management of an advisory board is one of the most subtle and complex journeys that a company will undertake. Done right, the process can lead to unexpectedly high growth rates. Done poorly, it is a waste of resources and senior management's time.

Chapter 5: Advisory Boards as Business Development Engines – The Beginnings

A well-constructed and professionally managed advisory board can bring amazing benefits to a company. A poorly designed and managed one is usually a colossal waste of resources. The difference often lays not so much in the idea of an advisory board, but in the execution of that idea by the senior management team, and particularly the CEO. In many cases, the productivity of a company's board is an indication of the effectiveness and sharpness of focus of the senior management team.

In order to show you how it can work, I want to describe the very first advisory board that I built specifically as a business development engine.

My fourth company taught me how to leverage the needs of a client base and fund the launch using customers' money. Beyond a validation of my suspicion that:

- a promising solution to a major problem would draw investment from those who will most benefit (the customers) and
- involving potential clients intimately in the process of developing solutions to their challenges would ensure their support of the company which then offered those solutions,
- another important lesson was learned - this time quite by accident. This was the company that showed me how an advisory board, if appropriately structured, populated and managed, could radically improve performance.

We had taken up the challenge to revolutionize the way feature films were financed in the US. Once our solution was perfected and business model was in place, we set about managing three flows. The first was the flow of product - film projects that we could finance. The second was the flow of investment dollars which would ensure that we could meet our obligations under the financing agreements. The third was the flow of bank funds to finance the balance of the production budgets.

Informally at first, but then more formally later, we formed two working groups that eventually merged into one advisory board. The first group was representatives from the film industry and their bankers. Their task was to organize the flow of investment ready opportunities. The second group was senior representatives of the Wall Street investment banking houses and big accounting firms. Their task was to organize the flow of investment dollars. Initially we spent time working to balance the flows but soon realized that, if we brought both groups together, we could more closely coordinate the process. Thus the advisory board as business development engine was born.

What was neat about this approach was that entire, multi-million dollar transactions were often proposed, negotiated and funded during single advisory board meetings. The process wasn't entirely on automatic pilot but it sure was a lot easier to manage than shuttling back and forth between camps. My team provided the meeting coordination, processing and the post-closing management - we also acted as the coordinator of the overall process and made sure that each interest within the group was fairly served. In the end everybody had a big win and everybody had a respected role in the process.

On reflection, there were at least three major characteristics of this advisory board that were important to its success. The first was that the board had a very well defined and obviously important function to serve. (And I am not referring to driving the run rate of a startup company.) When the members came to the meetings there was an anticipation of 'doing business' and 'getting things done'. As a result meeting preparation was very through, materials were provided well in advance and meeting participation was very active.

A second characteristic was that all board members had specific economic interests that the group would help advance. All of the players came to do business and trusted the others (including members of my team) to come to the table in the same spirit - a culture of cooperation towards a common set of goals that served the individual goals of each participant.

Finally, all discussions were conducted in a spirit of camaraderie and common purpose. Complex settlements would be explored and reached at the table and not left to extended phone discussions that typically involved lawyers and accountants. In other words, the decision makers made the decisions (and compromises) together.

From my team's perspective, the advisory board made life much easier. The flow of product, investment funds and bank loans was all organized within one venue. The regular meetings of the board provided a continuity of process that helped to organize a complex situation. Because the 'market' had become so well organized and the 'players' were all recognized 'friends', the process of arranging and closing financing became 'rationalized' - much of the uncertainty had been removed. My team got the credit for doing that and the company was seen as a necessary part of the process.

In the middle of the Big Apple we had organized a lower stress oasis.

Advisory Boards

Chapter 1: Turbo-Charged Business Development

My discussion with a CEO or Chairman about designing, building and managing a board generally begins with an initial contact which has been the result of a recommendation by a friend or business associate. Most often the recommendation comes out of a discussion about the lack of effectiveness of the company's business development efforts or the revolving door that has become the company's senior business development slot. During the initial call I usually recommend that the person read several of my articles on advisory boards and then call back if they are still interested in talking.

I confess that I make this suggestion purely out of enlightened self-interest. I want to cull out the instant gratification types who see the process of designing, populating and managing a productive advisory board as relatively simple and straightforward. If they will take the time to read and think about the articles, I take it as an indication that there is some hope that they are serious about engaging in ways that I have found necessary in order to produce a highly productive board that will drive the company's top line.

For those who call back there is yet another set of hurdles before we can discuss an engagement. I have learned that there is real benefit in running through a meticulous description of the process in person. It is important that the CEO or Chairman clearly understands what they are signing up for. Later is no time to realize.

What follows is a typical presentation in which I outline the dynamics of the process, a typical engagement and the areas that need to be thought through very carefully before embarking on the effort.

Parts of my presentation will vary with the size, complexity, scope and intensity of any engagement. But this should give you a fairly good idea as to what is involved. So join me over lunch in a meeting with John Slate – the CEO of Rocket Science, a fictional company that has been in business for about a decade and is currently doing roughly fifty million dollars annually in gross revenue.

It's not normally such a monologue, but I'll streamline it for you. For purposes of brevity, I'll skip the initial pleasantries and descriptions of the menu items selected! But I will have a well-crafted martini and do think that food is not suitably dressed without wine. This is how our first meeting went:

Lunch with John Slate

John, I appreciate your interest in my advisory boards and your willingness to sit through a description of what is involved in setting one up. One thing I have learned is that preparation is a critical part of the process. Another is that the company, and particularly the CEO, needs to have a good grasp on what is involved as well as what impact a board can have on the future of the company.

I'm not a golfer – never found a decent recipe for those little white balls – so I fish instead – but I'm told that a key to the game is preparation and practice. It is much the same with designing, populating and managing a board. I want to give you a fairly detailed briefing on what is involved. Some of this may seem tedious but I have found that going through it face-to-face and answering your questions afterwards is the best foundation for any engagement.

First and foremost, I want you to understand that this is an extended, complex and subtle process. You need to come to see that because sometimes tensions arise with CEOs who are anxious to get started - want to race through the 'getting ready' stage and get right to the 'getting people on their board' part. For this lunch, we must slow down and get your mind around the process – so that you can understand clearly what is involved and the foundation that needs to be created before a board can be launched.

We will need to make a baseline assessment. Rocket Science is not ready for a board and there is much preparation necessary to get it ready. You have built a magnificent company that is very good at doing what it does – but managing and benefiting from a business development advisory board is something else again.

Building a board prior to completing the foundational work would be like dropping a Ferrari engine into a VW frame. Without a good bit of re-engineering, pop the clutch and you get a pretzel not a race car! This is what potential advisors would see John and, in our experience, it is almost impossible to get high-potential members to make the kinds of commitments that a board requires if they see a train wreck as one of the likely future scenarios.

In the broader context, advisory boards are dangerous undertakings because the barriers to entry are so low. Any CEO can form one and most, at one time or another, try to. You could probably form one in an afternoon if you so decided. The trick is not getting a board set up it is setting up a board that can be highly productive when measured against a set of pre-established and agreed on metrics. In this case the metrics are focused on driving the gross revenue of your company. They are very easy metrics to set up and monitor but harder ones to have a board meet.

Like most CEOs, you suffer from several limitations that reduce your chances of success. First, although you are very good at the business of your business, your experience with highly productive boards – how to design, build and manage them – is limited. Second your range of contacts with potential members is also limited. Our experience is that you need to contact close to a hundred candidates to fill one seat effectively. Finally, you are very close to the trees and could use a set of eyes that is looking at the forest – a strategic view that can give you a holistic handle on the thing. An effective advisory board will impact – and place burdens on – every part of Rocket Science. But its members will also give you that long view that is so critical to your company's future.

Here is something that you need to think about. We will eventually be dealing with very sophisticated, experienced, well-connected individuals who have had careers that often involve building and managing businesses much larger than Rocket Science. John, they know good management when they see it. They will have built and managed very successful teams. We will be asking them to risk their reputations by becoming strong advocates for your company – reputations that they have spent a lifetime carefully building. For them this is not just a consequential matter – it will be the central matter in their thinking. In every discussion they will be looking for indications that you and Rocket Science may drop the ball - not follow up effectively on the opportunities that they can bring to the table – and they are very good at spotting those weaknesses. You will be dealing with pros at the top of their game.

Remember we are talking about building a board which will subject its members to a strict set of performance metrics. Members will be expected to produce. They will want to be sure that neither you nor the company – either through ineptness, inefficiency or poor organization and resourcing – will interfere with that performance. And John, trust me, simply saying that you 'won't' won't make any difference to them at all!

One of their security blankets will be the fact that you have brought in a set of professionals - steady and experienced hands – that they trust. One of the reasons that I formed the Council of Advisors is to let Members develop relationships with me – let them get to know my model. They have to buy into the model before we are willing to place them on any particular board. Many of them will have had seats on non-productive boards. Most will have decided not to waste their time like that again. It helps give them confidence that the process is being approached professionally and with careful planning and execution.

After listening to all of this, you may decide to try this on your on – and if you do, *mazel tov*. But at least listen to what I have to say. It will help you assess the risks.

If you rush through this or do it badly, you will lose - and end up doing much damage to the Rocket Science brand. Lots of CEOs have never thought of the negative branding that resulted from an unproductive board. But it is there - and the more influential your advisors the more broadly the negative branding will spread. That's right John, the better the people you have on your board the more pervasive the consequences of screwing up. A couple of 'A' list advisors and a botched capture effort can turn Rocket Science into the proverbial 'dead man walking' long before your realize it. Even talking to very influential people has a severe downside if you haven't done the necessary spade work first.

So John, let me outline the early stages of a typical engagement. Once an agreement has been inked, we begin an initial phase – not this lunch but a series of sessions in your office with you and your senior team. This stage has two principal objectives. The first is to thoroughly acquaint your team with advisory boards, the effort and commitment that will be required, the likely schedule that the engagement will follow, the relevant costs and benefits of the effort and to outline the terms and conditions of an extended engagement.

Secondly, I conduct a detailed assessment of your company, its history and resourcing and the potential benefits of building and managing a board for it. Successful graduation from this stage requires both that the company is ready to proceed with an engagement and we are convinced that the company is a good candidate for a board. This stage normally will take about a month to complete.

At the end of this phase, we begin an intensive effort of creating a design for your board. We work with your team to identify key targets for business expansion – both within existing business areas and into new ones. We also work with other team members to rework your materials – particularly the ones that will be presented to potential advisors and will be used by them in approaching targets. Very often CEOs have told us that this process alone results in a completely new understanding of their business – a collateral benefit.

This results in a preliminary design for a tailor-made board, a description of the various seats on that board along with a profile of ideal members, a schedule for populating the board, cost estimates and a plan for the resourcing and reorganization that the company must undertake in order to prepare for the launch. It normally takes two to three months to complete. So, you see we will have been at it for three or four months without talking to one potential advisor!

At the end of the first two steps, we will formally present our recommendations to you, members of your senior team, directors and other major stakeholders. Normally this is done within the context of a strategic planning retreat that covers related areas critical to the process of actually designing, populating, launching and managing the board. The result of this step is an approved plan and an expanded engagement agreement.

Once the design of the board and the profiles of members are agreed on, we work to find candidates for each seat. Two to four candidates for each are normally identified. Background information on each candidate is presented to you and your senior management. We then facilitate a meeting with your team to prioritize prospective candidates.

Once candidates are approved, I arrange for initial interviews. These interviews tend to be two-way streets with the company getting to know the candidate and the candidate getting to know the company and its senior team. Either can decide at any point that discussions should not proceed.

A major milestone in this process is when at least three board members have been identified, been offered and accepted seats and are ready to begin service. At this point planning can begin for launch of the board. The process of filling out a four to seven member board normally takes four to seven months.

While board seats are being filled, there is plenty that your team will need to be doing. It is vitally important that the company and senior management prepare for the launch and operation of the advisory board. This is not something that can be done 'on the run' John or 'after the fact'. Board members who experience an unprepared team will quickly re-think their evaluation of the company and the risks to their reputation. The recommendations presented and agreed to during the strategic retreat <u>must</u> be implemented by your team prior to board launch.

So John, now we are getting close to the launch. Once a sufficient number of members have agreed to serve on the board, we will schedule and organize an initial meeting. I will handle the arrangements and facilitate the meeting. You and your team will undertake the substantial work that needs to be done in preparation. Generally it will take about a month or two to prepare for the meeting. The first meeting of any board is critical to its continued success.

We have found it a good idea to coordinate a first meeting with either a strategic planning retreat or an all-hands retreat. My experience in facilitating these meetings will go a long way to assuring that the board will be launched successfully and make major contributions to the company's future - but your team will carry the substantial part of the burden.

Prior to the meeting, your team will have worked with each board member to identify targets of opportunity. It will be important that each member be involved in targeting at least one major source of business by the time the first meeting occurs.

OK, John – we're almost done – thanks for hanging in. A board normally meets four times a year. Two of the meetings are face-to-face - with one of them coinciding with the company's annual strategic planning retreat and the other occurring roughly six months later. The other two meetings are normally teleconferences.

But most of the work of the board is done via direct contact between individual members and the company's senior team – that means you and your most senior associates. Work, sometimes on a daily basis, with individual members to target, pursue and capture significant revenue opportunities will be your principal focus with the board. From our experience, you might end up spending as much as half to two-thirds of your time working with an active board. The percentages will be higher for your business development team.

While you and your team are working with board members, I will be managing the board. We will continually assess member's productivity, search for new members, advise you on the expansion of the board and on a whole range of other issues. We will facilitate meetings and conduct regular debriefings with each board member.

Well John, that's it in a nutshell. Take some time and think on it. Visit my website and read the articles posted there. And, when you are ready, let's schedule a meeting to answer any questions and decide if we are going to do this.

Summary

So John leaves with lots to think about and probably a decision to re-read some of the articles on the website. His senior team will be introduced to the idea of an advisory board and receive reading assignments as well. Time will tell what he decides.

My experience is that one in three decides, after such a lunch, to begin immediate discussions about having me build a board. Of the other two, half come back within six to nine months for the same purpose. In a serious way the process filters out those who would not make good candidates. Not bad for a pleasant lunch!

Chapter 2: Benefits and Costs

After thinking about our last meeting for a while, John came back with a series of questions:

What results should I expect from having a board and when should I start seeing them? What form will these benefits take and how will we be able to measure the value of them?

What will the board cost us to run and how should I put those costs in context? What are my fixed costs going to be? How about my variable costs? Could I really end up paying an advisor more than I pay anybody else in the company – including me?

Tell me more about what changes we need to make in Rocket Science? What personnel changes am I going to have to make? How about resourcing changes? You mentioned that the culture of my company and focus on business development efforts will have to change – how and on what schedule?

What will be the demands on my time, my team's time and the resources of Rocket Science? It sounds like the board could take a lot of our time. How should I judge the wisdom of making this time and other resources available?

Tell me more about the ongoing management of the board by you. What areas will you be handling and why shouldn't we manage them? Is there going to be an end to the engagement?

What will it cost me to have you design, populate and manage a board? What are my upfront commitments? You mentioned an expanded engagement agreement. Under what conditions does that happen and how much more will it cost me?

Some Necessary Preliminaries

We reached an agreement on a preliminary engagement and met at one of my favorite bars for after hour drinks. Initially John wanted to meet at his office. He said that he might want some of his senior team to sit in on the session. But I suggested that we have a couple more meetings one-on-one before involving others. That would give him a chance to get his mind around the value proposition and process before introducing it to other members of his senior team. John agreed to this. So I selected a bar where I had taught the bartender to make the perfect martini. Here's how it went:

John, you have obviously been doing a lot of thinking about advisory boards and our discussion over lunch last week. I suggest that we focus this session on two areas that you raised – the benefits and costs of having a board – and leave the others for later. My experience is that a more detailed description of the underlying value proposition will help you decide if further discussions are a good idea.

Before I launch into a description of the benefits, I need to cover some necessary preliminaries. These are issues that are so foundational to having an advisory board that, without your complete understanding of them, much of what we will do might be ineffectual. As we both want to avoid that outcome, let me quickly review four points. (At this point John took out a pad and started making notes – an action that always tells me that I am being taken seriously – and a good indicator of things to come.)

First and foremost John, <u>real change is going to require real change</u> and there is no way around it. By that I mean real change in the way you see the world and operate within it, the way Rocket Science is organized and resourced and the way your team functions – just to name a few. You can't have a productive board and expect that the future will be just an extension of what you are already doing. In this case the past is prologue only in the sense that it will become a reference to the way you and Rocket Science used to operate.

Change needs to begin with you and members of your senior team. But it will affect everybody in your organization and you need not only to see the need for those changes but to accept and commit to them. They will go hand-in-hand with preparation for launch of the board. Effectively done, they will radically improve the chances of success. Poorly done, they will confuse your organization and turn the board into a liability. In short, things must change and your ability to manage these changes successfully will be a major factor in the benefits and costs calculation.

Second, part of the reorganization and resourcing that we will be doing will be focused on <u>clearing the decks</u>. An advisory board will require a great deal of time and attention from you and other members of your senior team. A board is not an ATM – where you put in a code and take away money. But the time you spend with board members has the potential to generate returns that will drive your business to a new level. It will be time well spent.

You are going to have to clear a substantial part of your calendar for work with the board and individual members. Your head of business development will have to as well. You should expect to spend as much as half your time working on developing the leads that they generate, overseeing the development, red-teaming and presentation of proposals and for meeting with individuals that members will want you to get to know. That percentage will increase dramatically when you are on the trail of a specific chunk of business.

The reorganization and resourcing work that we will be doing prior to launching the board will, in part, be focused on clearing the decks in preparation of the kind of action that the board will generate.

Third, we are going to <u>design and implement a plan for shifting the focus of the current resourcing patterns</u> within Rocket Science. You are not going to need the middle-level business development types currently on your payroll. In many cases they will become more a liability than an asset. But you will have to step up your game substantially when it comes to preparation, red-teaming and presentation of proposals. And the capture process will have to work at a very high professional level. In short, we are going to have to prepare Rocket Science for the pressures that will come when the board shifts into high gear. Remember, the end game is not getting opportunities – its winning business. That means closing on the target, bringing it down and dragging it back to camp for processing. Real winners manage the entire process seamlessly.

<u>This resourcing plan will go farther than you might anticipate</u>. We are going to have to look at the entire corporate

infrastructure as well as sales and marketing. You will need the demonstrated ability to quickly and professionally expand your workforce – to keep track of rising levels of business – and manage accelerating change. A culture of professionalization is going to be necessary - and it has to be in place before the board is launched – potential board members will demand it.

Benefits

So now let's turn to some of your questions. John, your first set of questions was *"What results should I expect from having a board and when should I start seeing them? What form will these benefits take and how will we be able to measure the value of them?"* These go to the heart of the value proposition of an advisory board. Let me go through the major benefits that Rocket Science will realize as a result of successfully taking advantage of a board.

I'll start with an intangible benefit – branding. Yes, there are major benefits in having recognizable names (celebrities) on your board and that is a type of branding alright. But it is a different matter altogether when influential individuals are willing to aggressively represent Rocket Science to decision makers. Your company immediately steps up to a different level. You should start seeing these benefits as soon as you kick off the publicity campaign to announce the board. The more coverage you get that links these influential people to Rocket Science the better. You should notice an increased level of interest in your company and improved brand recognition among the decision makers you are brought in contact with.

Second, board members will be bringing you opportunities to capture new business that you would not normally have. Those opportunities will represent larger chunks of business - helping you to accelerate your rate of growth. You should start seeing these opportunities begin to fill your pipeline in the early months after board launch.

Additionally, board members will help you expand existing areas of business – to get more out of the positive beachheads that you have already established. You should see an improvement in prospects in established areas of business almost immediately.

As I indicated during our lunch last week, each board member should be targeting at least one major source of business prior to launch. While it will take a while to completely fill, you should see your pipeline begin to fill up with larger chunks of potential new business. Monitoring this flow will give you an idea as to how well the board is performing.

Third, you will be brought in contact with <u>a wider and more powerful set of individuals</u>. Remember that board members will have had very successful careers prior to joining your board. Part of their contribution will be bringing you and Rocket Science in contact with influential individuals and organizations which will help you grow.

You and your team will need to manage these new contacts very professionally. Some of them will be sources of the proverbial low-hanging-fruit while others will take longer to develop into sources of business. But you will need to spend part of your time cultivating these relationships – in concert with board members, of course. Here you can keep track of the <u>expansion of the range and increase in quality of your contacts and the contacts of your senior team</u>.

Forth, you will gain a group of <u>strong and influential advocates for Rocket Science</u>. Board members will be acting as advocates not just introducers. Your ability to work with them and effectively take advantage of the doors that they will be opening will be tested in the early stages. The first set of metrics will focus on how well you and your team are establishing those relationships but later on, once you have mastered that process, they will shift to how well you and your team are converting initial contacts to productive, working relationships. The board should be an <u>ongoing source of an expanding network of highly productive relationships</u>.

Fifth, you should see a <u>more effective targeting, proposal development, red-teaming, capture and processing of new business</u>. That means that Rocket Science should be pursuing larger and higher quality opportunities. But that's only the beginning. You should see a radical improvement in the quality of your proposals and a higher win rate – meaning that your proposals should be more effectively targeted to the needs of the potential client.

Sixth, you and your team will benefit from the <u>wisdom and mentoring</u> which will take place because of your close contact with board members. Remember, these individuals will by-and-large have successfully built and run organizations much larger than Rocket Science. They will have experiences that go beyond yours and those of your senior team. Their combined judgments and wisdom can be a resource of incalculable value to you and Rocket Science. It will be up to you to take advantage of this resource.

Finally, a well-managed and productive board will be seen as a significant asset when it comes to <u>valuation of your company</u>. When we get to the point of talking about exit strategies, the fact that you have influential individuals who are committed to effective advocacy will be seen as a major plus by any strategic buyer.

Costs

OK John, now let's turn to your questions about the costs of running a Board. *"What will the board cost us to run and how should I put those costs in context? What are my fixed costs going to be? How about my variable costs? Could I really end up paying an advisor more than I pay anybody else in the company – including me?"* I think that was the way you put it. So let me outline the various costs associated with designing, populating and managing an advisory board.

Let's start with the planning phase. I charge a retainer for the design, population and management of its boards. Costs are going to vary depending on size, complexity and intensity of the board required.

A typical retainer would be somewhere between two and four thousand per month for the early, planning stages and four to eight thousand per month for the latter stages. For Rocket

Science those numbers will probably be somewhere in the middle of that range.

The first phase of our engagement will involve two stages. The first stage will continue until the advisory board has been designed and a plan for work within Rocket Science has been agreed on. That plan will include issues like resourcing, expansion of your team and revisions of materials. At the end of this phase we will present our findings and recommendations.

The end products of the planning stage will be a design for the board, a detailed description of each board seat and profile of the ideal member plus a plan for getting Rocket Science ready for the board. The planning stage usually takes between two and three months.

Once we have completed this stage we will begin <u>the implementation phase</u>. We will begin the search for board members and you and your team, with our help, will begin the process of preparing Rocket Science. John, I can't make the point too strongly – it is going to be critical that you and your team implement the plan that we agree on. That implementation is usually the proverbial critical path.

Working with Advisory Boards and The Council of Advisors, I will identify a list of candidates for each board seat. We will conduct the necessary background checks and acquaint the candidates with Rocket Science. In some cases we will ask you or members of your team to meet with candidates. This is a process of getting acquainted – and it is definitely a two way street.

It's going to take a minimum of six to seven months to complete the plan and identify the candidates for your board. Once we get at least three who you have accepted and have accepted an offer to serve, we will begin planning for the first board meeting. The second stage of our engagement ends with that first meeting.

Now let's talk about how board members get compensated. Members will receive a retainer, an honorarium for meeting attendance and a reimbursement of out-of-pocket expenses. In general, and for a board of six members, the total costs in these categories will amount to what you pay one middle-level business development type. That's right John – six high powered advocates for the cost of one middle-level employee.

The biggest part of board member compensation will come in as a result of an incentivized agreement under which they will receive payments which are calculated based on the dollar amounts and quality of revenue they are instrumental in helping the company capture. That means that they receive payments <u>only if Rocket Science actually wins new business</u> – and the more new business the more they will get paid. So to answer one of your questions directly, yes you could end up paying a member significantly more than you earn in any given year. But I think you will be able to live with that – you will want them to do it again and again won't you?

And John, for board members who serve longer than one year we generally recommend that you offer them a chance to build a small equity stake in the company – generally in the form of warrants or options – nothing major but we have found that it generates a sense of loyalty to the company and will be seen as a recognition of their value to Rocket Science.

So that's how the board members get paid. To wrap this up, here is how I get paid on an ongoing basis. I serve on each board that I construct. I am responsible for the board's smooth operation, the assessment of member effectiveness, replacement of ineffective members and the expansion of the membership. For this service, I receive the standard board member compensation package – but no incentivized compensation agreement. In addition, I receive a retainer for an ongoing search for new members – either to replace existing members or to expand the board.

Check Please

Well, that's it John – the benefits and costs – at least to the level of detail that after hours drinks, a couple of very fine martinis and a good cigar will allow. I'm sure that you will have questions about what I've told you. I suggest that we gather again and this time focus on the balance of your questions. I also suggest that we focus on what it will be like to work with the board – how your world will be different.

With that John went on his way and I stayed to enjoy the last of the martini and another cigar.

Chapter 3: John's Questions – Round Two

John and I scheduled a third session to discuss the balance of his questions and the changes that will be necessary within Rocket Science to accommodate and take advantage of having a board. We met over dinner at one of my favorite eateries. This is how it went:

John, last time we discussed the benefits and costs of an advisory board. I want to give you some time to ask any questions that have come up as a result. Then I want to move to the balance of the questions you posed after our initial lunch. If that's alright, why don't you start?

John's Turn

Thanks Chief (a nickname) – I appreciate your time and patience. Mostly consultants try to close a deal during the first meeting – a real high-pressure sales job that I tend to resent. I appreciate that you have taken a different approach. After our first two sessions, I am beginning to see why you are cautious about entering into engagements. This is major surgery and the patient clearly has to be very healthy, eager for the procedure, clearly understand what is involved and be ready and able to make the necessary commitments. Sorry for the medical description, but it puts things into sharp relief for me.

One thing has stood out in my mind. You said that *"real change requires real change."* At first I admit that I thought it was just a trick with words but the longer I thought about it the truer it came to seem. We will not be playing around the edges with an advisory board and all parts of Rocket Science will be affected by having one – starting with me!

I've thought quite a bit about what it would be like to have five or six very well connected and successful people on the board – what it would mean for me and my focus. I believe that I now know why you spent so much time on this. These people are going to expect me to have time for them and to follow up on the opportunities that they can provide. You're right – I will have to clear my desk and prepare for this.

I also understand something of what you were getting at when you said that the culture of Rocket Science needs to be professionalized. I had drinks with a friend who is part of the senior business development team of a large company. They have an advisory board that does something similar to my version.

First off he told me that the board was a source of substantial new business on a regular basis. Then he started to sound like you – only maybe a little less articulate and focused. He said that most of his time is spent interacting with board members, following up on their introductions and shepherding the responses. At first he underestimated the time requirements and tried to operate on a business-as-usual basis. But one of the board members backed him up against the wall and explained the world to him.

But the second thing he said – and this is the one I wanted to mention – was that the member told him in no uncertain terms that his proposal development, red-teaming, presentation and capture resourcing was totally inadequate and that he had better step up his company's game ASAP – before he embarrasses himself and board members.

I took that as a serious bit of information – I still remember the look on Bill's face as he said it. They almost lost their entire board over this.

Finally, I now recognize that the changes in resourcing within Rocket Science will have to be pervasive and necessary for supporting and taking advantage of a board. I don't see the details of the changes at this point but I do see their general outlines and understand that they will be necessary prior to actually launching the board.

John's Questions

Let me get my notes from our last session. (As I mentioned before, I like people who take notes. It means that they haven't been spending all their time waiting for their turn to talk!) Oh yes, let's start with branding. I understand what you are saying about improved branding but how does Rocket Science take advantage of it? We are a private company that is not affected by public opinion – so public relations is not something we spend much time on.

Good question John. The branding that I am talking about is focused on the decision makers who directly affect the chances of Rocket Science winning new business. Most CEOs and almost all PR firms focus in an unfocused way on too broad an audience. Branding is important if it helps facilitate a positive outcome of decisions that really matters.

OK, I'll accept that. You said that the board will be a source of *"opportunities to capture new business"* that we would not normally have. How will that work?

The identification of new opportunities will be the focus of board meetings (four a year) and a good part of your time with individual members. You will be leveraging the members' contacts and reputation. Their willingness to make introductions and act as advocates will be critical to the success of the board.

But, remember that a board and its members do not constitute an ATM – you are going to have to work to build relationships based on trust – the stronger the relationships the more and higher quality the opportunities that will result.

I'll buy that. I sometimes wonder if Rocket Science, my team and I will be good enough to earn that trust.

You can't cower in the shadow of Mount Rushmore, John. You will need to find the stiffness to engage with these people and set expectations, metrics and drive the agenda. Believe me they will expect it and be disappointed if you don't. The short answer is that you and your team <u>have</u> to become good enough if this is going to work.

Also remember that nobody will accept an invitation to join your board unless they are convinced that you and your team are up to the challenge. The mere fact that you have a populated board will be an indication that at least they think you are worth the effort and exposure.

OK, that's a bit daunting in and of itself. Let's move on. I accept your suggestion that Rocket Science will become exposed to *"a wider and more powerful set of contacts"*. I also buy into the proposition that the board will constitute *"a set of strong and influential advocates for Rocket Science"*. The kinds of people you have described and the way the relationship with each of them is to develop virtually guarantees that. I understand that converting these assets into new business will require *"a more effective targeting, proposal development, red-teaming, capture and processing of new business."* I hope that we can talk a bit about what that means.

Before that, I want to visit two other points that you made. You said that one benefit would be the *"wisdom and mentoring"* that I and my team would have access to. Could you say a bit more about that? Also, you mentioned the effect of the board on valuation. We are not planning to exit Rocket Science anytime soon, but valuation is something that I think about. Could you say a bit more about how a board might affect it?

Sure John. First, mentoring relationships have evolved within all the boards that I have constructed. Most members are in what I call a grandfatherly mode – meaning that they value the chance to give back to the next generation the lessons that they have learned. If you are open to it, at least one of the members will begin to work with you on your management style and decision making. Others may partner with your business development team to help them raise their game. It happens naturally enough and is an additional benefit – one you receive just by being in contact with the kinds of people we put on a board and are open to receiving their help.

Valuation is a matter of perception as much as the numbers. You have to see your company through the eyes of a strategic buyer not an accountant. A company that has attracted the kinds of people that would be on your board and has negotiated the pro-active understandings with them that go with my board will be seen as having significantly more value than one that has an ordinary, mostly unproductive advisory board. The latter is almost always taken as an indication of failed management with appropriate discounts applied.

That's what I thought you would say. It is up to us to make this work. I remember you once saying that *"you can lead a horticulture but you can't make her think."* It's going to be up to us – my team and me - to think and act – to realize the value that is there to create.

John lets deal with your earlier question about more effective targeting, proposal development, red-teaming, capture and processing of new business. How are you and Rocket Science going to have to change the way you are doing business?

Your larger competitors have a highly developed process for identifying business that they want to pursue. You need to begin to emulate them. Targeting will be more focused on the core competencies of Rocket Science – what you are really good at. You will need to start sifting out the good targets from the red-herrings much more aggressively and effectively.

These competitors also have a more finely tuned proposal development and red-teaming process. Rocket Science needs to up its game in these areas. You will need to play like the pros – and deliver like them as well. One early advantage of the board will be that you will have a potent resource to guide you in this process – but you must make significant progress on the evolution of the corporate culture and capabilities before launch. Members will expect that you recognize the difference between what you have been doing and what you need to do to compete more effectively.

One of the principal challenges of winning larger chunks of business will be getting the organization up to speed to actually deliver. We will be focusing on the infrastructure – those areas which are critical to your company's ability to do that. There will be greater stress on HR during major ramp-ups. Your accounting and reporting systems will need to be looked at. Contract compliance, which you are already good at, will have to be beefed up. I think that you get the idea.

I am beginning to. Let's talk about the process you outlined. You described a planning period – getting ready for having the board – designing it and developing a detailed description of each seat on the board and the ideal occupants. As I remember, you said that would take between two and three months. My team and I are anxious to get going on this. Isn't there some way to shorten the planning period?

John, I'd like to say that there is but I would be misleading you. This is a complex process that requires careful planning and extended focus. SWAGs are not going to do anything but get you in trouble. And that's what you end up with if you try to phone in or short-circuit the planning process.

One of the most time consuming parts of this stage will be designing and implementing plans for refocusing Rocket Science. There may be significant changes required in your management team – most often we end up adding very experienced people in key areas. There will be new support systems to put in place – your CRM will have to be beefed up, for instance – and the new systems will have to be tested before launch of the board. As I mentioned in the last session, almost all of the materials that you now use in your business development efforts will have to be reviewed and most will probably have to be revised. I can see by the look on your face that you are realizing that this is a major undertaking. Keep that look in mind, John because that is exactly what this is.

Well that was sobering! I know that you have said these things before but that certainly got my attention. I think that I am beginning to realize how big a change this is going to be and why you are constantly counseling caution. Ok, let's say that it is going to take three months – now I suspect maybe more. How much time are we going to need from my team and how do we go about organizing them?

First off, John you are always going to underestimate the time required. For these two to three months you should think in terms of a dominating agenda. That means that you are going to have to let your people in on the process you are going through – tell them something about the board and why it will be very important to the company – and get their buy-in to supporting the process by helping to clear up your calendar. In the long term this will be therapeutic beyond just this project. Letting people in and asking for their help should be a major part of your management style.

Once you have made the arrangements for clearing your calendar you will need to meet with other senior members of your team. They will need to be briefed on the approach and their commitments to the process will be a key to its success. For them, as well as you, it's going to be immersion learning. Figure that this will dominate their lives as well as yours for the foreseeable future. We need to get it right and the only way I know to do that is to bear down and focus.

Once we begin to get the outlines of the board and reorganization plan, things will get even more complicated. We will begin to involve others in Rocket Science. That circle will grow until virtually everybody is involved.

Sounds like a pretty intense two to three months.

It will be – more intense than you can know. But we are talking about the very future of Rocket Science and everybody connected with the company. You and your team will be stretched and challenged. This is strategic stuff, John.

You talked about the relative costs of having a board – fixed costs about at the level of one middle-level business development type as I recall. What will be the impact of the board on the company? Will it cost us more or less to do business development this way?

It will cost you more. But not as much more as you might think. You will replace the middle-level business development types with a board. You will also beef up your targeting, proposal development, red-teaming and capture resources. There will be investments in new systems and the process of getting everybody up to speed. Your calculation needs to be a cost/benefit one. The question is *"if I make the investment in a board, will it pay off?"* Now before you look for a quick answer to that question, we will need to get through the planning phase.

One output will be that kind of analysis tailor made for Rocket Science.

You have said more than once that I will have to change my approach to the CEO role. What do you mean by that?

Change in an organization comes either with the leadership of the founders or over their dead bodies. Organizations that need to grow always prefer that the head person lead the charge towards change. The problem gets even more severe when you set on a course like building and managing an advisory board. My boards are not only powerful business development engines – they are also powerful agents for change within a corporate culture.

The biggest initial stresses come on the senior management. You and your team cannot continue to do business as you have. Delegation becomes a key skill. The strength of your judgment about people sits at the very center of the process. You must pick the right people for the right slots and then leave them to do what they are skilled to do. Micro-management will go out the window or you will go out with it. The days of dabbling in HR or financial reporting or quality control will be gone.

You must come to see your company in a larger vision and your role in a narrower and more focused one. As a CEO you can no longer be 'chief-of-everything'. Your leadership will focus more on choosing the right people and making sure that they have the resources for success. So you will become part quarterback and part water boy!

And what of my team - how will all of this affect them?

Those that can grow with the company – meet the needs to professionalize the culture and their performance – will survive and thrive. Others will decide that they are more suited for the relatively open but higher risk environment of a start-up and will depart for what they see as greener pastures. Some may fight the process and need to be shown the door – insisting to the end that you have sold out the very soul of Rocket Science. The thing about other people, John is that you don't get to write their lines – only your own. Your task will be to give them every chance and help to make the transition.

You are sobering today Chief. I think I need a drink.

Well, John you are in luck. As it happens this is one of the few remaining civilized places in a sea of rancid political correctness. By that I mean that we can enjoy a very old and smooth whiskey and I can combine mine with the pleasure of a good cigar. I suggest that we adjourn to the bar.

Chapter 4: Change Management

After getting well settled with a pair of uncommonly good single malts and a fine cigar, this is how it went:

John, I hope we have covered the questions that you had as a result of our last session. Let's move on to the balance of the questions you posed after our initial lunch. As I remember them, they were:

Tell me more about what changes we need to make in Rocket Science? What personnel changes am I going to have to make? How about resourcing changes? You mentioned that the culture of my company and focus of our business development efforts will have to change – how and on what schedule?

What will be the demands on my time, my team's time and the resources of my company? It sounds like the board could take a lot of our time.

Tell me more about the ongoing management of the board by you. What areas will you be handling and why shouldn't we manage them? Is there going to be an end to the engagement?

Personal Growth

John, let's start by talking about the changes that you are going to have to manage within Rocket Science. Remember my maxim – real change requires real change. You can simulate real change by simply moving the flatware around on the table but the effort will turn out to be a kamikaze raid on a vacant lot. The kind of changes that I am talking about are fundamental and strategic – purely tactical or virtual responses will only derail the process.

What do you mean by that, Chief?

Your overall goal is to grow your company and that involves seeing to the process of its maturing. Think of your company as your child. It is growing up before your eyes and you are doing your very best to see that it gets what it needs to grow in healthy and empowering ways. Now it needs to develop more of its own persona and become a young adult. You've got kids John. I'm sure that you know what that's like.

I sure do – but I never thought of myself as the parent of Rocket Science.

In a foundational way you are, John. As a parent, you have been responsible for keeping Rocket Science on the upward path, protecting it from its own excesses - seeing that it matures into a young adult that is widely recognized as a productive and welcomed member of society. Think of this process in two parts – efforts to make Rocket Science the best it can be and efforts to make Rocket Science a very productive and well accepted member of the larger community of companies.

Your company needs to develop the maturity that comes with age and experience. Its internal culture will evolve and expand to include skills and resources that were not particularly important in the early years. Other tendencies will be put away as remnants of a more child-like time. And your role as parent needs to evolve also. You won't be able to make all the decisions for Rocket Science any more – a real crisis for most parents!

Believe me; I know what you are saying. I get that feeling almost every day now. Simpler days brought lots of work that others now do. I sometimes feel like I am losing control – or, worse, becoming irrelevant.

You are in a way losing control – but also gaining new control at the same time. You can't be relevant in the terms you used to be. The company has grown beyond that. You can't relate to a teenager in the same way as you did to a three year old. But the new relationship can be richer and far more satisfying to both.

As I mentioned before, the existence of an advisory board tends to accelerate the rate of cultural change in any organization. A board populated by very experienced, successful and well-connected individuals comes with a lot of direct experience with that 'mature culture' that Rocket Science needs to develop. Members will naturally expect the company to meet the dual standards of a mature individual and a productive member of corporate society.

The initial test comes as board members get to know you and your team. They will not expect you to be ready to run a major company. If you were, you would be. But they will pay particular attention to your efforts to grow your capabilities in that direction.

Members will judge not only who you are but who you are trying to become and your chances of successfully making the journey. Their willingness to expand their commitments to you and the Rocket Science team will be guided by their conclusions in these areas.

So, I and my team are on trial from the very beginning.

Let's not say *'on trial'*, John. Maybe *'on probation'* is a better term. Remember that these individuals will have made a decision to join your board – and that in itself is a substantial vote of confidence.

To be as direct as I can, you will be on probation and the judges will be vastly more experienced and knowledgeable about what it is going to take for Rocket Science to succeed. If you turn out to be all ego and smoke, they will flush the toilet and move on - mostly in disgust. If you pass muster, they will support you and begin to bring you the opportunities that are the underlying purpose of the board.

Board members will also be getting to know your senior team. It will be important that you set the tone for those relationships – leading by example. Your team members will watch how you interact with the board and how determined you are to grow personally. You need that determination to become contagious!

Personnel

Chief, you said a couple of times that I will have to be ready for major changes in the Rocket Science team. What did you mean by that?

When a company is in the early stages of growth you often have little to incentivized people with. Money is tight, equity is illiquid and career tracks are narrow and short. So most people in your position give titles – it is all there is that might mean something to the recipient. But there is a downside to this strategy and it starts to show up when growth complicates the challenges that each team member must manage.

Let's look at HR. In your early years your VP of HR could be a highly effective recruiter – in fact, that was probably the most effective strategy. But, as the company grew, the challenges that must be dealt with got not only much more complex but also much more potentially damaging if mismanaged. I believe that you are working through your first equal opportunity lawsuit, aren't you?

We sure are – and it's a real pain. I can relate to your point. It's becoming clear that our VP of HR is not up to the challenge. We have had to get lawyers involved across a much broader range of issues than I would have thought. The costs are running up fast. It seems we have not been in compliance with a bunch of requirements. The complaint is specious but our failure to cover key bases is coming back to bite us in the butt.

Sorry to hear that. If it helps, I have heard it before.

Doesn't much – but thanks anyway.

Another position that is often a problem as a company grows is that of VP of Finance. In the early years a controller was fine. But, as things get more complicated and start to come in faster and in larger chunks, things can get out of hand for less experienced people. I know that you have been bringing in a part-time CFO. How's that working out?

The difference has been noticeable almost from the very beginning. I had no idea that things had gotten so badly out of whack. But a couple of months of working with our new VP of Finance have brought things along. And Helen now knows what she needs to learn in order to be a real VP of Finance. She has decided to go back to school and we've agreed to foot the bill.

A very wise decision, John. You should give Helen and people like her every support if they are determined to grow with the job. Some of your people won't make the journey with you. Others will, and you should support them.

Resourcing

Now let's move on to the question of resourcing. As I mentioned before, you will need to change some of the resourcing patterns within Rocket Science. For one thing, you will not have to spend so much on your junior-level business development team. But you will have to increase investment in proposal development, red-teaming and capture.

One suggestion that I have is that you need to review the performance and qualifications of your head of business development. I'm not sure you have the right person in that slot. Remember, I said 'not sure'. Clearly there has been significant success in that area. I recommend that I spend some time with Linda and give you my recommendations.

I'm pretty happy with what Linda has been doing. She is the biggest supporter of you and the idea of a board. You should spend time with her. You'll see her as a strong ally.

I think I have a pretty clear picture in this area. I have already started to think about how to make the changes. I'll admit that it seemed pretty daunting at first but, once I sat down and got my mind around it, the planning went much better.

Good – I'm glad that you are working that set of challenges. Some of our heaviest lifting in the early stages will be developing and implementing a plan for reorganizing Rocket Science and getting it ready for the board.

Cultural Changes

Last time we talked about how the Rocket Science culture was going to professionalize. Do you think that you have a handle on that?

I'm not sure. I've been talking about 'professionalization' with some of my friends. I've sure gotten a range of reactions from them. Some see the point immediately and talk about how I need to let it happen and up my game to keep pace. Others look at me with something approaching horror and end up asking *"how could you let that happen to a great company like Rocket Science?"*

As you know, I talk to lots of people about major challenges that I'm facing. I've found that it helps me get a clearer picture of the options and better choose the right path. But this one is all over the map. Why is it that the very idea of professionalizing a corporate culture seems to draw such a range of reactions?

There is an ancient Chinese proverb that might help here. Among all dragonfly larva there is a blood oath that the next one that goes through the barrier will come back and tell the others what it is like. But it has never happened. Why?

Probably because dragonfly larvae live in water and when they cross the barrier they become air breathing insects.

Yes, that's right. The larvae cannot live in air – it is a mortal threat to them. But neither can a dragonfly live in water. What was once a sustaining environment is now a death trap. Some people live their lives avoiding the process of professionalization. For them the very thought of such an environment is threatening. Others have made the journey across the barrier and the very thought of a less-than-professional culture offends their sensibilities. You can tell a lot about somebody by engaging them on this issue.

But, that aside, you have to decide whether you are willing to allow the Rocket Science culture to professionalize.

You once said to me that change in an organization either occurs with the support of the founders or over their dead bodies. I've thought about it and have decided that I would rather survive the process. By the way, that cigar smells pretty good and you look like you are really enjoying it – got another one?

Time Commitments

Sure John – here. That decision alone – if you can stand by it – earns you one. Now let's talk about time commitments. You asked *"What will be the demands on my time, my team's time and the resources of my company?"* The initial stages of the planning process are going to be very time consuming. We will need to be methodical in our analysis and planning. You are right to conclude that, once up and operating, the board will take a lot of your time. Investment of time in the process will yield benefits in proportion to your ability to make that time available and to constructively and creatively engage with the board.

We will have to pay a lot of attention to adjusting the load within Rocket Science. We don't want to simply pile more onto the backs of you and your senior team. It's not just the time commitments of your senior team that you need to pay attention to. We will need to shift some burdens onto the desks of others. Delegation of responsibility and authority is going to be a big part of the process and a major focus of our planning.

A lot of time will have to go into explaining the process and its implications to key people. We will need buy-in from those people who are going to have to pick up delegated responsibilities. We will need to help them understand what is going on and why their world is changing so much. All of this needs to be put into the context of your vision for Rocket Science.

And what about the demands on our resources – particularly capital resources?

Building a board is a lot like planting a crop, John. As I said before, an advisory board is not an ATM – where you put in a code and get back cash. You will be forward investing in the board – just like a farmer prepares the field, adds fertilizer, plants the seeds and tends the field. The success of any board depends on how well you engage in each of these activities – how good you and your team are at farming.

Your pre-launch investment will be in the cost of the engagement, the time invested by you and your team and the costs of materials and events that are associated with the process of designing, setting up, populating and managing the board. In addition, because there will be a sales cycle involved, you will have to carry the board until the first revenue check clears.

The decision to launch a board is a calculated one based on a judgment that initial investments will yield very substantial benefits down the road. Advisory boards are not for those insisting on instant gratification.

My Role

OK – let's move to the final set of questions. You wanted to hear more about the ongoing management of the board by me

I have found that, particularly in the early years, it is a good idea for me to stay involved in the management of the board. There are six major areas that we work in.

The first is the facilitation of the developing relationships between board members and the Rocket Science team. It is important that this goes well. It sets the tone of much of what is to follow – it either limits or expands the potential of the board. Our participation as a facilitator and honest broker will help you and the board members navigate the shoals and reefs of the early months. If a disagreement arises, I will mediate.

Second, we provide the organizing center of the board. We communicate with members about how things are going and whether their expectations are being met. In this role we can serve as a kind of early warning sensor net – getting you and your team information about stresses that are developing or opportunities that are being missed.

Third, during the first year I chair the board meetings. We make sure that the agendas are well formed, that each member is contributing. Our participation helps you and your team to learn to handle the process of managing the board.

Fourth, I facilitate review and training sessions for your team focused on how to work with the board. I also identify issues as they arise and work with all parties to resolve them. My objective is to give you a smoothly working and highly productive advisory board and to help you learn how to maximize your returns from it.

Fifth, I lead the process of assessing the performance and contributions of each board member. I arrange for replacements in the event that one is needed.

Sixth, I take the lead in expansion of the board. When we get to the point of adding seats, I will identify and qualify additional board members.

Why Management by Me?

As I recall your last question was *"What areas will you be handling and why shouldn't we manage them? Is there going to be an end to the engagement?"* Well, to answer the last question first, my involvement will end the moment that you feel we are not adding value to the process substantially in excess of the cost of that engagement. We are always aware that the decision to continue is yours.

We do insist that Rocket Science commit to an initial period without reservation. But at any time after that you can simply end the engagement by notifying us. Our belief is that we need to be generating so much value that you will not even think of saving the money and spending it somewhere else. We are dedicated to being the highest return investment that you make.

I manage boards on an ongoing basis for three reasons. The first is based on experience with many companies. Preparing a management team for dealing with 'Mount Rushmore' is an art. I have seen normally confident CEOs go into vapor lock when confronted with a board. The stakes are simply too high – both for you and for my reputation - to trust that process to fate or chance.

Secondly, as the person that has formed the board, I have a different relationship with board members – I have more leverage as a source of possible additional postings. I also can have conversations with board members that would be hard for you and your team. My approach can be more direct.

Finally, I can maintain the strategic – top-down view of the battlefield. I bring a perspective into the mix that is from above the fray.

Engagement

Well, John – that's it in a nutshell. You have the whole crop. Nothing left but to decide. Here is an agreement for our initial engagement. You'll notice that it is only one page long. We like to keep things simple where we can and the agreement is one of the few places where we can. Take a read through it. When you are ready to go, sign it and send a copy back to me.

After taking a few minutes to read it through, John signed the agreement and handed it back.

I'm ready to go now, Chief. You'll have your first check delivered in the morning. Let's plan a kick-off session for next week.

We spent the rest of the evening in small talk, another martini and a second cigar.

Planning for Two Journeys

Chapter 1: The Keys to Change Management

Let's take a break from the narrative to talk a bit about some of the terms I've been using. The principal components of change management as I'm using them here involve:

- professionalization of a corporate culture,
- restructuring and re-resourcing of an organization, and
- restructuring and augmentation of a management team

An over-arching issue is the implementation and monitoring of the change management plan. These are very complex and subtle processes. They must be closely coordinated. To go back to a previous example, it is like deciding to put a new, more powerful engine in an old car frame. You must prepare the frame for the forces that it will experience with the new power plant. The board is the engine while all the rest is the frame – context must be as well managed as the new engine.

A change management plan for the organization and operation of an advisory board focused on business development will touch all parts of an organization. The company in all its aspects must be well prepared by the time the board stands up. And there is a very good reason why this is the case – aside from the fact that it is the sensible thing to do. The context must be prepared for the introduction of people who have great experience with building and managing larger and very successful organizations. Without adequate preparation, they will be less enthusiastic in their support of the company and will worry about its ability to deliver. This kind of 'friction' needs to be avoided. Careful and thoroughgoing preparation is the way to do that.

There are significant downsides to poor coordination and implementation. The biggest ones can be grouped under the heading of negative branding. Building and standing up an advisory board is a high-profile undertaking. If you screw it up, lots of important people will know! Additionally you could end up wasting precious resources and dissipating the enthusiasm and momentum that brought the company to the point where it can benefit from an advisory board.

Because the risks are so high, change management is <u>the</u> major challenge to a management team looking to stand up an advisory board. Most often the attention of an outsider serves to make sure that the plan is not only drawn correctly but effectively implemented. Management needs to make sure it is not glossing over opportunities in the rush to get the board into operation.

I recently worked with a company that wanted a board badly. The CEO had read some of my writings on the subject and decided that a board would help him grow his company. We reached an agreement and started work. About three months into the engagement, the CEO realized just how much work needed to be done in preparation. As a result, we finished a rough reorganization plan and suspended the engagement until he could prepare the company adequately. This kind of thing happens regularly. I am sure I will build him a board but it will probably be a year or more before both he and the company are ready for it.

Professionalizing the Corporate Culture

Professionalization describes a process which is part science and part art. In this context, it describes the evolution of a corporate culture from talented armature status to that of experienced and proven pro. Think of it this way:

Jack Harris was a talented quarterback for Nowhere State. He led his team to a state championship three times during his college career and in his final season they were undefeated. The take on Jack was that he could pick a defense apart.

So the draft comes and Jack gets picked early on. When he shows up to training camp for his first pro season, he is full of himself and confident that he will quickly assume a leadership role on the team. But experience quickly disabuses him of that expectation. Jack comes face to face with a widely recognized fact. In football offensive players generally mature during college but defensive players take a bit more time to come into their prime. Jack was playing with amateurs in college. Now he is playing with pros. The defense is just better. They are picking apart his offence. What Jack got away with in college just doesn't work with the pros. He is going to have to lift his game substantially to even just survive.

The same is true with corporate cultures. When an advisory board is put in place there are two sets of pros that enter the field. The first are the board members. These are very experienced people towards the ends of their careers. They know how the game is played and what it takes to win. Members also tend to be very good judges of human potential – and how well individuals are living up to theirs. For the most part, they are quick, decisive and unerringly right. They are a group that can unnerve a quarterback!

The second set of pros is the higher-up decision makers that the company will be put in contact with by board members. They will not be presenting to the 'flack catchers' anymore. If they don't raise their game, they will brand themselves negatively. And, at that level, one negative branding goes a long way.

Here is an example of what I mean. I built a board for a company that did a lot of business with the Navy. The senior team was used to making extended initial presentations to junior officers – presentations that often did not generate any subsequent business. That was before the board was put in place.

One of their new board members was a retired senior flag officer. He made arrangements with a couple fellow admirals to introduce the company to the 'E' ring of the pentagon. *"You are going to have fifteen minutes."* Was the way he described the scheduled meetings. *"You've only got two weeks to prepare for it. You better get cracking."*

After his message sank in, we went to work with the senior team. They distilled their value proposition and quals down to the point that they could be delivered well within the time frame and still allow for Q&A. Their presentation focused on the business that they wanted to bid on and connected the value proposition and quals directly to the client's needs.

We practiced delivery over and over and brought in members of the red-team to role play the admirals. The result was that they could deliver a high-powered message in a very short time – no nonsense, no irrelevancies and *nae daffin*!

The point is that the standards and expectations of these senior people are going to be substantially higher than the company is used to meeting – and their audience's fuse is going to be much shorter in the face of people who just don't seem to understand who they are talking to and what the situation demands. It is no place for amateur behaviors. Many times the team needs to draft some experienced players and help their stars move up just to deliver what is expected. In the end they need to be seen as understanding what is necessary and then doing what is necessary to deliver it.

As a culture professionalizes, there are behaviors which simply won't work in this brave, new world. Much of what passed for management during the cottage stage will be experienced as inadequate and inappropriate. Reporting patterns, fuzzy overlapping of authority and responsibility and back passages to top management will have to be re-examined and mostly replaced. The garage-stage tendencies, like the toys of childhood, will have to be left behind as the organization matures.

The best way to kick a professionalization program into high gear is to bring in senior types with lots of experience and knowledge. These 'grains of sand' can serve as the stimulus for the pearls. As mentors they can add a whole new dimension to the corporate culture in a relatively short time.

Restructuring and Re-resourcing the Organization

I often describe this process as re-dreaming the company. It involves seeing the company in an entirely new way. Often I suggest that the senior team do a bit of reading about complexity theory as an antidote for the post-Fordist perspectives that have most often dominated their thinking. The suggestion that it is productive to look at a company as a complex self-organizing entity – a living organism with its own needs, tendencies and appetites - is often a radical idea at first. But I highly recommend the perspective – particularly during efforts at accelerated growth.

Capabilities and enthusiasms which sustained and drove forward a company in its early years will no longer be sufficient. Like a growing child, the company's needs change – the list of resources that are critical change – the drives evolve – the institutional knowledge has to expand.

One of the major requirements in this area is the redefinition of roles, authority, responsibilities and prerogatives. It's not just that new job descriptions need to be evolved and implemented (they surely do) but the new structure has to serve the needs of a rapidly growing company – one that is moving from adolescence to adulthood! The organism is growing up. Management needs to both get out of its way and see that it has what it needs to grow.

As it grows its needs evolve. As new resources are integrated into its mix, the balance of resources at its disposal also needs to change. This is particularly true when you add an advisory board to the mix. Here are a couple of examples:

The business development team will almost certainly need a major overhaul. Most companies use middle-level executives in the front-line hunt for new business. With a board in place, there needs to be a decreased emphasis on the middle-level business development types. At the same time the resourcing of proposal development and capture areas will have to be expanded substantially.

As a prelude to bringing a board online, the corporate infrastructure almost always needs to be beefed up. Two areas which ordinarily need the most work are human resources and financial control and reporting.

HR will come under increased pressure on a number of fronts. They will have to deal with much more substantial increases in the workforce over a much shorter time horizon. In some cases they will be asked to deal with an entirely new requirement – the need to have people 'on the beach' – ready for deployment. As the organization grows quickly the knowledge, systems and experience needed to manage HR will increase.

Unfortunately as organizations grow the possibility of lawsuits grows as well. HR is often one of the most poorly managed sources of corporate liability. This risk needs to be aggressively managed.

Financial control and reporting will often be in much the same situation. It is not just a matter of putting more sophisticated and robust reporting systems in place. The company will need a more complex approach to arranging for and managing financial resources. The need for financial vice president-level skills will become more acute. The CEO and COO will find less and less time to spend on these matters but will have a more acutely felt need to be informed about them.

Both of these areas need to be professionalized. After all, when you drop in a new, more powerful engine, you don't just upgrade the steering wheel – you need to do the same for the shock absorbers and breaks!

Management team restructuring and augmentation is always a major part of the preparation for standing up an advisory board. The first step is a careful and realistic assessment of the strengths and weaknesses of the team – not in terms of the current levels of business but under the pressure of the rapid growth that is being planned. The assessment is designed to identify those team members who will be able to grow along with the company as well as those who are probably not going to be able to make the journey.

Most organizations have these two types of employees in senior positions. Senior management needs to sort out both. I recommend an employee and team assessment as an initial step. These represent an inexpensive way to get a handle not only on the current capabilities of your people but their interests, potential and capability to grow. Once they are identified a company needs to implement an aggressive program dedicated to the education and training of these key team members.

It is hard to overstate the impact that adding sure hands trained through extensive experience in larger organizations can have on a company. People who are experienced with professional systems and approaches can bring with them knowledge and judgment that will help a company navigate the difficult process of accelerating growth. They will help the company up its game and play at the level necessary. They will also bring additional skill sets that are necessary to manage a rapidly growing organization. The balance between this 'new blood' and 'developing indigenous talent' is a major challenge that management has to meet and overcome.

As the team grows it is vitally important to deploy an integration strategy which will insure that cliques do not form – schisms within the team. Apart for the obvious reasons there is one that merits special mentioning. These very experienced new people will tend to act as mentors to others. That can seem a threat to the position of other members of the senior team – the CEO in particular. But these mentoring relationships will be a key factor in the ability of the company to manage the change needed to prepare for the board. You have to let them happen.

The change management plan needs to be a formal and holistic document – a reference that all parties can use to measure progress. It is important that it manages a seamless integration of the strategic and tactical. It also should contain very specific metrics for each component. The latter is very important because there will be conflicts over performance and implementation – tensions which will arise because of divergent agendas. There will be a lot of pressure. A well-structured and presented strategic plan will go a long way to easing these strains.

The implementation of the plan should be assigned to a team that draws from across the entire company – not just the senior levels. This committee should have regular review meetings and be able to engage in frank and direct conversations – it should not finesse any issue no matter how minor it seems at the time.

It should also be tasked to make sure that the burdens do not fall onto the shoulders of one or two team members – a very common occurrence in these situations.

Chapter 2: The Board Design and Population

Producing a well-balanced design for a board is part science and part art - but it is mostly science and diligent spade work. Board seats should be a reflection of the company's current strengths and future business development aspirations. The board should also be proportional to the company's capabilities. By that I mean that a three or four seat board might be all one company can handle while a six or seven person board would be manageable for another. Finally, the levels of reputation, experience, range of connections and activity of board members should be designed into it. A board should be tailor-made to a company's capabilities. One size definitely does not fit all.

The Design

The easiest way to begin the design of a board is to start with a detailed review of a company's existing client base. Particular attention needs to be paid to the potential for expansion of the beachheads that have already been established. Areas should be identified that show potential for extensive growth. The bulk of the initial board seats should be designed around these areas and support and extend the company's business development efforts. A limited number of seats should also be allocated to areas where the company is looking to expand – either in terms of new clients with existing products or services or entirely new additions to the product/service mix.

I start by identifying the most logical seats that a board should have. Each is described in terms of an existing client base, sales channel or product/service. These are the areas that the members will be asked to help with. In some companies this will be a particular segment of a government agency. In others it might be a type of sales channel. The goal is to rough out an initial design based on these areas.

Once the rough design is in place, we set about refining it. It is important to get the descriptions of the focus of each seat as detailed as possible. We develop a careful description of the knowledge, connections and reputation that an ideal board member would have. As these descriptions evolve we constantly visit questions of the depth and balance of the evolving board design, the characteristics of the ideal members and how we would actually stand-up the board – prepare for the launch and select board members.

Ideal Members

There are lots of people who would jump at a chance to serve on an advisory board. Most will either be unqualified or incapable of meeting their responsibilities. Many are interested because they consider it good for their resume. Others because the think that the board is going to be some sort of coffee clutch – a senior advisory committee. We regularly encounter wanna-bee CEOs who see the board as their chance to prove to the world that they know how to run a company. But these boards are not honorary and they are not advisory in that sense. Board members are expected to generate actual leads to significant chunks of business. They are required to be effective advocates for the company in the process of capturing business and they will be measured by a strict set of metrics which are based on their productivity. That means that they have to be the principal reason that a company gets a high quality shot at significant pieces of new business. If they don't perform they will be removed.

Ideal board members have five major characteristics. The first and foremost is that they clearly understand and accept the obligations that they will be assuming as part of the advisory board. I can't emphasize this too strongly. This understanding must be reached from the very first conversations with a potential board member. Later is too late.

Second, the potential member may be retired but it is important that they are not retiring. By that I mean that they may have left full time participation in an organization in exchange for a more flexible schedule but they should not be deciding how much work and how much golf - with the golf increasingly winning out. The ideal board member is a highly active and motivated individual who wants to make a difference.

Third, the reputation of a board member is always their strongest asset. The individual should not only be widely known in a relevant space but widely respected as well. They should be able to leverage that reputation in service to the company. Their highest focus should be its welfare. And they should not be seen as trying to monetize their reputation gratuitously. If their advocacy is seen as reflexively instrumental they probably should move into politics where that is the norm.

Forth, an ideal board member has a wide range of currently active contacts in the space that they are going to be targeting. This is one of those areas that need to be checked very carefully. Some contacts have a very short shelf-life. Others stay fresh for years.

Finally, it is important that the potential member be willing and able to make the kinds of commitments that participation will require. Board members need to be able to work closely with the senior team. They will be participating in a complex process of engagement, targeting, and capture and delivering on important pieces of business. Members will be asked to be supportive of others on the board. In short, they need to clearly understand what is going to be involved and just as clearly be capable and willing to fill the role.

The Search

The heart of an effective search for board members is a well-constructed network of senior recruiters and other people of influence. The net needs to be very widely flung on the one hand and very well focused on the other. Our experience is that we look at preliminary information on a hundred potential members to identify just one. That alone should give you a good idea of what we go through just to populate a six or seven seat board.

Of course, recruiters are not primarily in the business of filling board seats. There isn't enough money in it to make the effort cost effective and often the candidates are rather hard to find. Over the years we have developed broader-based relationships with recruiters which allow us to be more effective in the search.

Our value proposition to them includes the possibility of follow-on business and a compensation based on the first big piece of business that the member brings in.

It is critical that the search be both extensive and effective. Getting the right candidates and negotiating the right understanding with them are the keys to populating the board. The work is hard and sometimes frustrating. But this is no place for an easy way out.

The search process is also a major source of uncertainty when it comes to the time required to stand up a board. It takes as much time as it takes and the company needs to understand and accept that. At times we get lucky and completely fill out a board in a couple months. At other times we are still searching for the right person for a particular seat months later. The best we can do is to make sure the search is well based and designed and that we are diligently following every lead that is generated.

One major advantage that we have is that a growing number of recruiters now already know the basic requirements of service on one of my advisory boards. This institutionalized knowledge is invaluable as it allows them to pre-screen candidates. Some recruiters have increased their hit rate from one in a hundred to one in ten! You can imagine how much easier they are to deal with.

Identifying and Vetting Candidates

Once candidates have been identified the process of prioritizing and vetting begins. In many ways it is similar to vetting a potential member of the senior team. We are very interested in learning about the person – their skills, reputation, integrity, range of contacts, capabilities, intentions and suitability. I am also concerned that they understand very clearly what is going to be expected of them and that they are ready, willing and able to make the kinds of commitments that are required.

I conduct initial interviews and the early screening on behalf of the company. I start with a traditional CV. My next step is to identify those people who, based on that information, would seem to be good candidates. I then deliver an extensive package to them which includes information on the company, a description of the board, information on board membership – compensation – responsibilities and a package outlining the terms of engagement. I ask them to review the materials in anticipation of a tele-conference. The call is designed to answer any of their questions about the company, the board and their responsibilities as members.

The experience is illuminating in many ways. Somewhere around a third of the candidates decide not to go any further. It may be the first time that they come to realize that membership on an advisory board will be real work – and that is not what they are looking for. They may just decide that it will be too much work – taking too much time from golf. Or they may decide that, after years of calling the shots, they are not prepared to work in an advisory role and be subject to performance metrics. For whatever reason, they drop out of consideration.

For those that do survive this initial conference we call for references and engage them in conversations about the specific seat on the board that they would be invited to occupy. This phase involves the execution of a non-disclosure agreement (NDA) because considerably more detail is provided about the company and its relationships with existing clients. The candidate is asked to develop a plan for supporting the company's efforts to capture new business in specific areas. This plan focuses heavily on the connections that the person has and the possibility that they will be useful to the efforts. We use these plans as the basis for selecting candidates for meetings with the company's senior team.

Filling Out the Board

By the time we have identified a number of candidates we have substantial files on them. Our next step is to meet with the senior team and go through all the files. The meeting agenda involves a careful consideration of each one. The result of that meeting is a prioritization of the candidates and a list of additional information which the team needs to get ready for actually meeting with them. By the end of the session we will have a set of additional questions to pass on to the candidates.

The first introductions come when individuals are invited to meet with the CEO, COO and/or SVP Business Development. Most of the time these meetings are face-to-face. We very occasionally use video-conferencing when schedules are tight and distances great. My own preference is that these first meetings be quasi-social. They tend to be casual and without highly structured agendas.

Everybody already knows the basics of what they need to know about each other. It is now a process of filling in the blanks and gauging the chemistry. Much of the time is spent on 'how well do you know x' or 'what do your know about the y program' – and these conversations tend to flow in both directions. By the end of the meeting both sides generally have decided whether they can and want to work together. Our hit rate during this phase is very high – better than two-thirds of the candidates both pass muster and decide to go to the next phase of discussions. Of the other third by far most of them withdraws rather than are declined.

Generally there will be a minimum of two to three meetings with each candidate before an offer of a board seat is extended. These meetings will tend to focus on the candidate's plan for supporting the company and the integration of that plan into the company's business development efforts. If things go well, the result will be an offer of a seat.

We go through this process for each seat on the board. Multiply the number of meetings and the work required for one seat by six or seven – and then factor in that again for null results - and you will get an idea of how much is involved.

A major milestone occurs when we have at least three board seats filled. At that point we can begin to organize an initial meeting. It is time to stand up the board.

Now let's return to our narrative. The board has been in existence for about six months. We are about to deal with a major problem – the removal of a board member.

A Working Board

Chapter 1: The First Board Meeting

"John, I've got great news. We have our third board member - received the signed agreement this morning. That means that we are close to launch and can set a date for the first board meeting."

"That's fantastic Chief. How soon can we have the first meeting?"

"There's still a lot to do before we can actually bring them together. Your team is proceeding well with the reorganization and re-resourcing. We need a session with them to determine where we are in the process. If they can get things wrapped up within the next thirty to forty-five days, we could schedule the first meeting two to three months from now. That would give everybody adequate notice."

"Sounds good to me. I'll schedule the senior staff meeting for the end of the week. I'll also let them know that we want a detailed report on their progress and the possibility of completing the work within the next month."

Years later John and I still remember this telephone call as a turning point in our efforts to stand up the board. It was the first solid indication that all the work that had gone into organizing the board was beginning to pay off. It also shifted the process into a new gear.

Three members had signed on. That meant that we could begin the process of organizing the very first board meeting. It also meant that the senior team at Rocket Science would have to redouble their efforts to make sure that the reorganization and re-resourcing changes were going to be completed on time. John would also have to organize a meeting of the Rocket Science Board of Directors and shareholders. It was time to formally form the board.

I arrived an hour before the staff meeting with even more good news. Two more had accepted seats on the Rocket Science board. That gave us a full complement for the first meeting.

In Rocket Science's case we were able to put the meeting on one of my very favorite venues – a three-day cruise to the Bahamas. John, like many of the CEOs that receive this suggestion from me, had a somewhat incredulous initial reaction. *"That seems to me a bit of a boondoggle,"* he offered. But I explained that a cruise is an ideal venue - a controlled environment - in a way that no land based event is. I also explained that it is cost effective, more conducive to developing strong personal relationships and that the facilities on the particular ships that we select were head and shoulders above those that most land based resorts offer.

I showed John that the cruise would cost about 60% of the land-based options. That was enough to close the deal. So a cruise to the Bahamas it was.

Getting Ready

The staff meeting was a complete success. The whole team had been working very hard to prepare for standing up the board. They had come face to face with major difficulties and overcame them.

It was clear that the reorganization and re-resourcing work could be completed within the next month. I could see a great deal of pride reflected in their eyes. And in truth, they had every right to be proud. They had substantially reinvented Rocket Science in an amazingly short period of time. The Company had developed from the proverbial ninety pound weakling to a well-muscled athlete that was eager for the next challenge.

We had added three very senior individuals to the team. The money spent on middle-level business development types had been reduced while additional people had been brought in to beef up proposal development and capture. We had also organized a standing pool of very senior individuals for the red teams and a virtual network of experts to be called upon on an as needed basis. It was clear that Rocket Science would be ready to meet its new advisory board within the next sixty days.

A new Chief Administrative Officer (CAO) had been in place for a couple of months. Lois was taking large chunks of work off of John's desk. Her remit included finance, HR and quality control. Lots of senior time was being freed up.

About halfway through the staff meeting the focus shifted to preparing to work with individual board members. Two broad areas needed attention. The materials that would be provided to members for their use in their role as advocates for the company needed to be finalized up. Also plans had to be developed for working with individual members to target their first piece of business.

I had lunch with John. *"Well Chief, the pace is certainly picking up. I can feel my guys' energy levels going up – and my adrenaline is certainly working overtime. And, by the way, I'm starting to really appreciate the wisdom of clearing my schedule and those of my senior team. When you first told me that I would need to clear half my time for working with the board I thought that you are exaggerating. But after this morning's session I think you may have been too conservative."*

"John, wait until the afternoon session. Once we start planning for working with individual board members targeting specific pieces of business the pace is going to pick up even more. And wait until you finally start to do business with the board. They are a fast crowd. You and your team have been in training for this and I think you're ready for it. But don't be surprised if Rocket Science has trouble keeping up."

After lunch the group broke up into working groups with each focusing on a specific board member. They generated modified materials for use in approaching specific types of clients. But before we broke up Linda had a comment that set the tone for the afternoon sessions. *"I've already had calls from two of the board members. They wanted to let me know how pleased they were to be on our advisory board. They also began to sketch out specific pieces of business that they wanted to pursue.*

Fellas, we've got a tiger by the tail here and we better be as good as they expect us to be." The CEO nodded then added: "Actually we've got five tigers and we need to be quick as well as very good."

Meeting the Press

There were other activities that needed attention. The PR firm needed to get out a press release. They had been briefed on the advisory board and alerted that an announcement was imminent. We had already reviewed a draft release. Now we have the names to fill in the blanks. Rocket Science was about to get a heavy dose of positive branding!

It was also time for John to get himself Linda out before the media. With a spade work done, we were ready for interviews and radio and television appearances. The PR firm had organized a campaign complete with media targets and collateral materials. We arranged for board members to provide quotes for the press release. In one case a new member was interviewed by local media – she had her own PR firm! The buzz was on and every employee of Rocket Science seemed to be aware that something very good was happening.

The Sprint to the Quay

The time between the staff meeting and departure for the board meeting was high pressure for the team. They implemented the last bits of the strategic plan. They also finished work on the materials that the members would be using. We organized a teleconference to brief the new board members and provided them with a detailed agenda, information on the venue and metrics for measuring success of the meeting.

Two weeks prior to departure each board member received a detailed package which included the generic and focused material. They also received a full set of travel documents – including information on the ship, itinerary, ports of call and shore excursions.

Four days before departure we had a staff meeting to review the agenda, objectives, metrics and assignments. Everything and everybody was ready – time to take it to sea!

Departure Day

There's something about arriving at the quay and seeing the huge cruise liner that is going to be your home for the next few days. And there's something transformational that occurs when you cross that gangplank onto the ship. It is like the first steps on a journey to another world – definitely taking you outside the box and generating a feeling of expanding horizons and possibilities. No matter how many times I do it, I get the same rush.

The group assembled on the pool deck. They began arriving as soon as the ship opened for check-in. Most still had their 'land faces' on but I knew that would quickly pass. By the time they had a couple of drinks and a bit of steel drum music the relaxed environment began to work its magic.

We were a substantial clan. By the look on John's face I could see that he was realizing that a very potent group was assembling. All of the board members and most of the Rocket Science team had come with traveling companions. There was an air of excitement and anticipation and a flurry of toasts to the future of the company and the board.

By the time the group settled down to the first dinner I could see the beginnings of a real camaraderie emerging. Like Nero Wolfe, I have a rule about dinner – *"no business is discussed"*. Like Rex Stout's great fictional detective, I think that humans ought to talk about other things occasionally. So that first dinner was a social occasion – with people getting to know each other. Another of my rules came in handy – *"you can't sit next to your traveling companion at dinner"*. It always amazes me how much more active table conversation is as a result. So the Chief spoke and everybody complied. It was a wonderful experience – seeing a board come to life before my eyes.

Day One – At Sea

"Ladies and gentlemen, let's come to order. Some of us have a full schedule of work before us – and a full day tomorrow as well – others are eager to get to the pool. (Groans and clapping – I'll leave it to you to guess who did which)

That's how the day started. I gaveled the board into existence. During my initial remarks, I reviewed the schedule and objectives and described the non-business parts of the itinerary. There were shore excursions to consider and we had arranged a meeting in Nassau with some local business people. I also briefed the group on the ship, dining arrangements and provided informational packets to all. After that the traveling companions headed to the pool deck and the rest of us settled down to business.

The morning was dedicated to presentations by the Chief Operating Officer and Senior Vice President of Business Development. Both were tasked to deliver a summary of the preparations that had been undertaken and to review important materials. First up was the COO.

I never coach executives in these kinds of situations. My philosophy is that, aside from making sure that they don't hit the nuclear button, mistakes are a constructive part of learning. Well the COO, Don, made one right off. He came prepared with a forty-slide deck and proceeded to plow through it as if he was briefing a bunch of middle level managers. I think he got to slide number five before one of the board members shut him down.

"Look, we already know most of this stuff and don't need you reading these slides to us. You should have given us this deck before we arrived and we would have gone through it. That would have saved time and focused this session on the next steps. You need to pick up the pace Don. As I see it there are some basic things that we need to know. Let's focus on them."

The rest of the board members nodded in agreement. Fifteen minutes later the COO had a new agenda and an unused deck of slides. Here is the core of what the members were getting at:

"We can get you in the door and act as advocates for Rocket Science. But how are you going to make us comfortable taking that risk? How can we be sure that you won't mess up and loose the business - and damage our reputations to boot?"

By the end of that two-hour session it was clear to the team that the learning curve was going to be much steeper than they had anticipated. Board members were aggressively testing them and their preparations. The company was being held to a new and much higher set of standards. Mount Rushmore was speaking in very clear and forceful terms.

To their credit, they responded well. Where they had no answers they admitted it. They were clearly back on their heels. During the half-hour coffee break I met with them. The COO said, *"Wow, these old guys sure can set a fast pace. They don't mess around with pleasantries either. And they really seem to know what they are doing. I've never been through so much in such a short time."*

My reply was direct. *"You are getting a real time education in the way very successful people approach things. There is, as my Scottish ancestors would say, 'nae daffin tolerated here'. You did well to pick up the pace. Remember, most of these people have built and managed organizations much larger and more successful than Rocket Science. They are a fast crowd. Learn from them when something like this happens. Take their lead – they know what they are talking about. Take their concerns seriously. Engage with them as mentors that have already decided that you and your company are worth the effort. Remember, you are still on probation. Prove yourselves worthy of their trust!"*

The next session involved a presentation by the Senior Vice President of Business Development. In an attempt to simplify things Linda had thrown out her original slide deck and reduced things to a single slide. This is what it looked like:

> **Working with Board Members**
> 1) you get us in
> 2) we establish credibility
> 3) we respond to the need
> 4) we get the business

She got as far as the second point when one of the Board Members jumped in with *"Linda, when I get you into a meeting you'll have all the credibility you need to close the deal – you don't build credibility – you need to avoid losing it!"*

The resulting discussion focused sharply on the fact that each board member was determined that their association with Rocket Science would not damage their reputation in any way – that it would only enhance it. To her credit Linda took the point immediately – but then she had heard it once before that very morning!

The discussion then moved on to a reprise of the work that had been done in preparation of the board's launch. This was the first time members saw the true breadth of the board's potential. It was also the first time they had seen evidence of the dedication of other board members. The range was impressive and I could see a growing confidence on their faces.

The afternoon session was a presentation by the CEO. His remit was to focus on important Rocket Science quals, to introduce the new materials and to outline the basis for working with the board members. Early in the session the issue of the value of a certification came up. The company had received one that was prominently displayed on all its literature. A member asked *"what is the value of this certification to me as a client – other than making you more expensive and taking you longer to deliver?"*

The resulting discussion demonstrated a blind-spot that many companies like Rocket Science have. John was very good at justifying the value to other people who had bought into the certification regime. But these guys were asking from the perspective of a potential client. Preaching to the choir had no impact here. The question was *"what was the addition of the certification to the value proposition from the client's perspective."* As the session broke up it was clear that the senior team needed to develop an answer.

Later that night I came across the entire team. They had claimed a section of one of the many lounges on the ship and were earnestly working the problem that the afternoon session had presented. The COO summarized the group's focus. *"We had always taken as a given that the certification was seen as a good thing but we never looked at it from the perspective of a client. The Board has forced us to do that because they know it will be a major question in the minds of people they introduce us to. I'm convinced that it does add to the value proposition but we need to be able to communicate that effectively. We also need to realize that this has been, and will continue to be, a major concern in the minds of every potential client."*

John Slate added, *"I used to tell people that one of my strong points was that I looked at the world through the eyes of our clients. But the board has put us all to shame. They have the vision we need to gain."*

Day Two – Nassau

The morning of the second day found the ship in the beautiful harbor of Nassau. We were going to spend a whole day there. The traveling companions had already chosen shore excursions or decided on a day of shopping. But for the team and the board it was a day of work – with maybe a little time for play later on.

The schedule involved a morning series of breakout groups with individual board members to discuss specific pieces of business. Their task was to come up with a detailed plan for targeting, proposal development, approach, delivery and capture. These would be submitted to the whole group during an afternoon session.

During the afternoon session each member took the lead in presenting their plan. Key members of the team supported them. During each presentation other members would chime in with observations or offers of support through their own contacts. I could see that the mix was really starting to work.

My job was to monitor the presentations and keep an eye out for indications of weaknesses. I did see one member who seemed to be less aggressive than the others. Most would not have caught it but it did stand out to me and I made a mental note to have a one-on-one conversation. But for the most part things went extremely well. By the time the group broke up and headed for the quay we had detailed plans for approaching five major pieces of new business. I noticed that John Slate's feet did not seem to be touching the ground and the smile on his face was yards wide. Rocket Science had its working advisory board.

Day Three – Journey to a Private Island

Day three was given over to socializing. The itinerary had been chosen to allow a more social schedule if the work during the prior two days had come out OK. Morning found the ship at the cruise line's private island. It was time to play.

During my initial remarks I had suggested a volleyball tournament between the board and the Rocket Science team. That suggestion had been taken up so, with the help of the cruise director, one was organized. The board won – giving credence to Waylon Jennings' observation that *'old age and treachery always overcomes youth and skill.'* It was a great time and everybody was celebrating the work that they had done.

Lunch was in a private setting. I noticed was that the two groups had merged. The early tendency to sit apart from each other was gone. There was also an air of celebration – lots of toasts to the future and reflections on how far they had come in such a short time.

Day Four – Return to Port

The group that disembarked was very different than the gathering of strangers that met on the pool deck just three days earlier. There were real friendships developing. Board members had come to know and respect the Rocket Science team. They were even more committed to helping it grow. The CEO and his team had begun to realize the true depth and breadth of the resource that they had access to.

John and I shared a flight home. *"I never thought a cruise could be so productive or so packed with important things that needed doing. When you first suggested it I was afraid it was going to be a leisurely journey with little getting accomplished. This was a very busy time – with lots going on and much accomplished.*

The foundations are laid for a very productive working relationship with the board. I am excited at the possibilities."

I had seen a few things slightly differently. But that was to be expected. My job was to take the long view and anticipate challenges before they came into full flower. There were stresses that needed tending to. One board member looked to me like he was going to be a problem. And the Rocket Science team needed a bit of attention. But, for the flight, I let John bask in the glow of a rising sun.

Chapter 2: Conflict, Renegotiation and Removal

"John, we have a problem that you and I need to sort out."

The Need to Act

That is how our meeting began some six months after the board's launch. I had been monitoring the members during that time and it was becoming clear that we were going to have problems with one of them.

That is not to say that there hadn't been bumps along the way. An advisory board focused on driving the run rate is a complex organization made up of even more complex parts. There were stresses as pressures to deliver results increased. Sometimes, those pressures surfaced in non-productive ways. The Rocket Science team occasionally stumbled and needed to be brought back into line. But the board members were getting good at that and the team was responding well.

This was a different kind of problem altogether. This member just wasn't working out. He seemed fascinated by conversations about management and was often second guessing the CEO. He was increasingly unresponsive to management's requests for reports, support and new initiatives. He also had a high opinion of himself and his position in the world. But that wasn't converting into progress towards getting business. Now, he was beginning to disrupt the rest of the board and negatively brand the effort and Rocket Science. So John and I sat down to review options. This is how it went:

"John, I think that we're going to have to replace Dave. I see three areas where he is coming up short. First, despite my conversations with him, he continues to be convinced that his reputation is so strong that all he has to do is make introductions and the business belongs to the company. It is very difficult to get him to follow up or stay with the team as they pursue leads. He also continues to insist that introductions rather than advocacy are his appropriate contributions. His overblown sense of self-importance is clearly not subscribed to by those who he is introducing us to. His initiatives are not progressing. The value is not there for us.

As you know, I have just applied the metrics that we agreed to as a result of our six-month review of board performance. I have gone over the results of all members. Dave is the only one that did not measure up. When I reviewed these findings with him he became argumentative then defensive. He will probably not take the metrics seriously and will continue to just phone it in.

Second, Dave is not adding to the board meetings. As other members' efforts move us closer to actually capturing business, he has become more and more dismissive of them and their efforts. He seems to want to have the same conversations over and over again - probably to avoid admitting that he is failing in his obligations to Rocket Science and the rest of the board. This is having a mildly corrosive effect. I have had a couple of other members mention this. It isn't lethal to the board but it does potentially limit its effectiveness.

Finally, I got a call from a friend who asked me specifically about him. It seems that Dave has been talking out of school on us. Dave ran into my friend at a bar and he got an ear full. Our board member explained how neither you nor I really understood how the world worked and that the board was not going to work out. In addition to a failure of morality, this amounts to negative branding and we need to deal with it right away. This is your board not Dave's. If he is not prepared to live by your rules and within your vision then he should leave.

Despite our careful selection process and subsequent efforts to maintain a clear understanding with all board members, this one is heading south. I recommend that we replace Dave. If you agree, I request that you write a letter asking me to terminate Dave's board membership. If you do concur, we should move quickly."

John took a bit of time to reflect on my recommendations. "OK, Chief. The team has also had conversations about Dave and his lack of significant contribution. The truth is that he has become a sort of caricature of the 'bad member'. They are losing respect for him. The last board meeting put the difference between Dave and the rest of the members into high relief. I agree – it's time to make a move. Let's do it. I'll dictate the letter right away. How do we proceed from here?"

"It's pretty simple – not nearly as complicated as removing a sitting director. The agreement that we have says that Dave can be removed without cause at any time. He can also leave the board without explanation at any time. I will meet with Dave and let him know that the company has decided to terminate his membership on the board and offer him the graceful option of withdrawing."

"Will we have any legal exposure as a result of the termination?"

"No significant exposure, John. But we need to make sure that nothing happens to negatively affect Dave's reputation because of this. We are not out for retribution. This is simply a partnership that didn't work out. Our best option is to go our separate ways without recrimination.

It will be very important that neither you nor any employee, director or shareholder of Rocket Science engage in any conversations – public or private - about the termination – positive or negative. Dave will be asked to do the same. We will issue a neutral statement as part of the announcement of his successor stating simply that Dave has left the board. I will let him know about my conversation with Ralph – as we have some indication that he is talking out of school – and will ask him to cease. I will also make it clear that, if any of the initiatives that he has help start should pay off, he will be compensated according to the agreement. And that should be that."

I had a cup of coffee while John drafted the letter and passed it by the corporate council. The lawyer brought in the letter for John's signature and we discussed the marching orders for me and the Rocket Science team. I also reviewed the conversation that I was planning to have with Dave. John signed the letter. The next step was a meeting with Dave – one I was not looking forward to. But it was my job.

Prior to actually meeting with Dave I called each of the other board members and briefed them confidentially on John's decision. None of them were surprised at the turn of events. It always amazes me how much ownership most board members quickly come to have and how much concern they evidence for the welfare of the company.

Meeting with a Departing Member

I called Dave and suggested a meeting. At first he was resistive. I am sure that he suspected. But I was insistent and we decided to meet the next day.

"Dave, Rocket Science has decided to ask you to step down from its advisory board."

I wasn't sure what the look on Dave's face was meant to communicate. On the one hand it looked a bit relieved while on the other there seemed to be surprise.

"Might I ask why?"

"As you know, I have completed a performance review of all board members using the metrics that we all agreed to at the very beginning. I discussed the results of that review with you by telephone last week. Yesterday I delivered the findings to John and Rocket Science's corporate council. Their decision was to ask you to resign from the board."

"And what if I won't?"

"Then they will remove you under the terms of your agreement. Either way you will be off the board. They just wanted to give you a chance to take the initiative."

"What about the things that I have going?"

"Rocket Science will stand by its obligation to pay you in the event that business is actually gained according to the terms of its agreement with you. Further, the company will issue a statement indicating that you have left the board without any comment on the circumstances. It will be made simultaneously with the announcement of your replacement. If your replacement picks up any of your initiatives and generates business from them, we will split the fees between you."

"I would appreciate them not making a big thing about it."

"You can count on that. Additionally, the management team will be under orders not to comment on your departure in any way. I don't expect that they will be asked – but the bases will be well covered. There is one thing that I need to mention. As you know Doug Framer is a good friend of mine. He told me that you had a conversation with him in which you disparaged me, John and Rocket Science. I'm not interested in debating what you said. I am only making the point that the company is prepared to agree that this just didn't work out and part company. But, if they find out that these kinds of conversations are taking place, they will get very aggressive. The agreement which you signed specifically prohibits you from doing this kind of thing. Have I made myself clear?"

"Yes you have and I appreciate the directness. I did have the conversation with Doug and regretted it almost immediately. I will let him know that he should forget what I said because it is not true and I really didn't mean it. I guess I felt over my head on the board and ego got the best of me. Tell John that I apologize."

"I'll do that. Here is the agreement to withdraw. Take a read and, if it is OK, sign a copy for me. Your withdrawal from the board will be effective immediately."

Dave read the agreement and signed a copy. "I'm sorry that this didn't work out Chief. Maybe next time."

Dave paid the check and left me to enjoy the rest of my cigar. I never like these meetings but they occur regularly enough when you are dealing with something as complex as advisory boards. I headed back home knowing that the next meeting at Rocket Science was likely to be a far happier one. The board was getting ready to draw first blood!

Chapter 3: First Blood

The first 'big win' is always an emotional one for the management team and the board. It is a solid indication that what they have invested so much time and energy in is starting to pay off. This morning's teleconference was focused on what looked to be the first big piece of business that the board had generated. It had been in existence for a little more than nine months. They were getting close on a number of chunks of business but one in particular was very sweet. And it looked to come in first.

Rocket Science had a longstanding relationship with one client. They had had a number of contracts that extended over multiple years and were highly rated by the client as a valued provider. This good relationship had allowed them to gradually increase their business base. Several Rocket Science employees had offices within the client's facilities and there was a fairly constant dialogue about other challenges that the company might help with. The company/client relationship was close and very positive.

One board member had a positive impact on this already strong relationship. Mark Silver had a strong reputation in the space that the client served. He also had a number of professional relationships with senior executives of the client. Finally, he had a strong knowledge of the space and was seen as a visionary by many in it. His decision to hitch his wagon to Rocket Science was widely seen as an endorsement of the company and its management team. Rocket Science began to be known as Mark's guys!

Shortly after joining the board Mark launched a series of meetings that involved not only the senior team from the client but experts in the field. John Slate supported the formation of this group and Rocket Science served as its informal sponsor. The group came to be seen as one of the venues where quality thinking about the future was done – and the company benefited by being its sponsor.

One evening, Mark was having drinks with the CEO of the client. Mary Morris wanted to thank Mark for putting together the 'thinking group' and for the benefits that her company was realizing from it. They had been able to identify a new direction – another market application for one of their products. It was a major opportunity and Mary was grateful.

"I need to thank you for the work you did in putting together the Rocket Science group Mark. We have identified a major opportunity because of our participation in it – one that none of our competitors seems to have picked up on. We owe you and John big time. Thanks."

"Happy to be of help, Mary. Truth is that I've enjoyed pulling the group together. It has really stretched me out and got me thinking about new approaches to old problems. I can't remember when I've been so mentally sharp. It's like being back at MIT."

"Before we get misty-eyed about college days, I've got something I'd like to talk to you about. I know that you've been helping John and his team. They seem to have come a long way in a short time. There was sharpness about them that wasn't there before. I suspect that you and the other board members have had something to do with that. Some of the work they have been doing for us is considerably above their usually high standards.

We recently received a proposal from them on an extension of work they are doing for us. Mark, it was a sharply focused and professional piece of work. They touched all of the bases and hit the ball out of the park. We like the company and look forward to doing business with them – but this was a real bonus. John and Linda are on top of their game."

"The board has been running them pretty hard. I have been managing a red-teaming process that is at the pro level. But more importantly the team is really upping its game. It seems like every employee is determined not to let the company down. Board members have taken note. After a rough patch early on, John and his team have risen to the occasion. The company has also brought in some world-class talent. They have a virtual network of senior resources that is very impressive.

I'll be honest with you Mary. When I first went on the board I had one eye on the door. They were asking me to be a strong advocate – not just to provide introductions – and to put in a lot of effort to help them up their game. This approach to advisory boards was very new to me. Doc Smith put us in a real working harness and started cracking the whip. Recently he removed on of the members for 'non-production.' These guys are not playing around. The board is having a huge impact on the company and I feel like I have a whole new life to live. It is very energizing."

"I've heard that Doc is pretty good at cracking the whip. I'm not sure that I would have put up with it."

"Well, if you have the chance, give it a try Mary. You may get to the point where you want to get into what I am sure the Chief would call your 'grandmotherly mode'. I'll tell you one thing; it's a lot better than sitting on a bunch of mind-deadening boards. I wouldn't trade the experience for a dozen seats on ordinary ones. But you had something you wanted to discuss."

"Yes I do. We have a piece of business that is much larger than what we normally put out to Rocket Science. It is about a hundred million dollars over five years. In the past we would not have taken them seriously on something like this but now we are prepared to. But, before I let the proverbial genie out of the bottle, I wanted to get your recommendation. I know that you have a fiduciary relationship to Rocket Science and I don't want to ask you to violate that."

"Actually, that's not strictly true Mary. As a member of their advisory board I am bound to help them find and capture new business. But I don't have the same relationship with the company as their directors do. If I don't think they are up to what you have in mind, I'll tell you."

"Thanks Mark – that will help a lot. Anyway, this business is more central to our value proposition and we would be betting a big chunk on John and his team. I'd like to walk you through it and get your reaction to the possibility that they would be invited to bid."

Mary did exactly that. She outlined in detail the work required and its importance to her company. As friends, they were able to have a frank and open discussion of the possibilities. Mark was able to help her analyze Rocket Science's strengths and weaknesses – and to assure her that the weaknesses would be aggressively addressed by John and his team with close monitoring by me and the board. In the end, Mary decided to allow Mark to carry the news to John Slate – they were invited to bid on the business.

As soon as Mary left, Mark was on the phone to John Slate. *"You need to get over here right away. I have something you are going to enjoy hearing!"*

That was enough to get John's attention. He jogged the ten blocks from the Rocket Science offices to the bar. He knew that Mark was well a serious player on the board. As cryptic as his call was, John knew that good things were afoot.

"OK, Mark what's up. You look like the proverbial cat that just swallowed the canary!"

"You might say that John. I just had a session with Mary Morris. She wanted my opinion on something and I was more than pleased to give it to her."

Mark reviewed his conversation with Morris. He could see John's eyes getting bigger as he talked. After a detailed description of the weaknesses that the Rocket Science team would have to address, Mark got to the punch line. *"It's yours to bid on John. Just make sure that Rocket Science doesn't screw it up."*

The rest of the evening was spent roughing out an action plan that included proposal development, red-teaming and presentation. The also developed a plan for dealing with Mary's concerns – identifying changes that would have to be made in order to get the company in a position to win the business.

That evening was the first step in an effort that resulted in Rocket Science submitting what was sure to be a life altering proposal for the company. In the end they beat out their competition and the scuttlebutt was that they were about to win the business.

Two of Mary's concerns merit mentioning here. The first one dealt with Rocket Science's ability to ramp up its workforce fast enough to deliver under the contract. The HR department had responded with an aggressive but plausible plan that had been a central part of the proposal and a big factor in their win. Mary was also concerned that John's company might not have the internal resources to adequately supervise the work. Mark and John put together an oversight plan that drew on key resources in the Rocket Science virtual network.

The business was won and the run-rate of Rocket Science was increased by forty percent overnight. The board had made its first mark – they were in the game.

On Leadership

My conversations with CEOs often turn to the question of leadership. This is particularly true with those who have taken seriously my suggestion that they might have been the principal limiting factor in the growth of their organization. Generally I focus on both the positive and negative behaviors which define a leadership style.

The good CEOs take these conversations very seriously and I have seen many of them make remarkable leaps of maturity because of that. It is important to remember that it is the founders that have to take the lead in this process. Board members will help them along the way but it is up to the principals to make and keep the commitment to grow in ways that allow the company to mature. The next two chapters focus on two types of behaviors – one that empowers and another which limits growth. Hopefully they will start you thinking about ways that you can improve your leadership style.

The final chapter in this section deals with the challenge of building and managing a balanced senior team. One of the critical issues is how well the CEO envisions then constructs that team. It should be a constant focus throughout the process of building, standing up and managing a board.

Chapter 1: Leadership That Empowers – The Fire of the Mind

> 'Give a man a match and he will be warm for a day,
> Set a man on fire and he will be warm for the rest of his life.'

Hidden deep within this adolescent obscenity lays a fundamental truth about the nature of leadership. The fire in this case is, of course, the fire of the mind. It can be kindled, for instance, when an individual first experiences how much they have to contribute to a team and, if they set very high standards for themselves, how excellent they can really be. These lessons learned are among the greatest gifts that any human being can help another acquire. Personally I mark these lessons learned and taught as among my greatest gifts received and finest contributions made.

I am often struck by how many successful leaders are highly effective teachers - and struck even more by how the lessons that they teach result in changed lives and kindled, or rekindled, fires. The teams they build often set themselves apart with superior performance and seemingly impossible accomplishments.

A story comes to mind about a man who rose to high political office. Afterwards he found himself running his own company and dealing with a young associate whom he had tasked to produce an analysis of a critical part of a major assignment. The young associate submitted his report and it came back heavily marked up with comments - 'this is not clear', 'are you sure that this is the case?' and 'I'm not sure that you got this right', etc. The final mark was a rather direct suggestion that the report needed to be further researched. The associate redoubled his efforts and submitted a substantially revised report - only to get it back with a slightly reduced rash of similar comments and queries. What followed was an all-night effort at improvement.

The next morning he walked into his senior's office and dropped the report on his desk. *"Sir, I have worked all night on this. It is the best I can do. If it's not good enough, I guess you'll have to fire me".*

"This is the best you can do?"

"Yes it is!" came the reply.

"OK, now I'll read it."

The report ended up playing a critical role in the successful completion of the assignment and the associate learned the difference between what is casually good and what is purposefully excellent. Two lessons were forcefully deployed. First, 'if you are going to work for me, I expect your best first time and every time'. Second, 'you are capable of much more than you allow yourself'. One lesson without the other would not have been nearly as effective.

The elder had seen unrealized potential in the young associate (an important skill of any effective leader) and structured a learning process that allowed him to directly experience how great his potential really was (a critical skill that often puts potential on the road to reality). A fire had been lit.

An effective leader not only kindles these fires of the mind but connects them to a humanity that tempers bravado. The really good lessons come not only with a sense of empowerment but also with a profound sense of humility that banishes shame in favor of a kinder, and often whimsical, relationship to one's self. In that combination is the beginnings of true human growth.

Learning how to kindle and tend these fires should be a top priority for any CEO (or CEO to be). It is always one of the primary areas of focus in my CEO coaching engagements. The skill is central to good leadership.

Think of it this way, as a leader it is always better to develop a team of maturing adults than one made up of insufferable, angry, prideful and resentful adolescents. A team of the former can change the world: a team of the latter will most often end up destroying each other and your company.

There is a second characteristic of enlightened leadership that I would like to highlight. At a recent event, Bob Woodward told a story about a lunch he had with Katharine Graham. The Watergate articles had begun to draw fire from the administration. The Post had, in deciding to back its reporters, put its journalistic reputation on the line. The situation was tense. The two of them sat down to lunch in Mrs. Graham's private dining room. The first question she asked was *"when are we going to learn the truth about what really went on?"* As Woodward told it, he answered *"probably never"*. Katharine Graham looked at him intently and said *"don't ever tell me never"*. As Woodward put it, *"I left that luncheon a highly motivated man"*.

Good leaders have a way of generating large effects with seemingly small efforts. The trust that she had in her people was evident in the Post's willingness to go to the line for them. Her message was 'you are capable of turning never into now'. And that they did.

It is important for every CEO to spend time on a regular basis identifying the opportunities for teaching (and learning) such lessons - and thinking honestly about how they either took advantage of, or missed, the chance to kindle a fire. I realize just how difficult such an objective assessment can be but the results can be well worth the effort. First to the benefits:

Three come immediately to mind. First, the review will produce a remembering that is not tainted by the 'heat of the moment' - a forthright review of where leadership skills either rose to the occasion or fell short of the need. Done with an openness and affection for human frailties, such an analysis can help a leader grow past their own limitations. Second, the process can result in a re-thinking of attitudes towards various team members. Missed opportunities can often be re-found - fires that should have been fanned can now be tended and nurtured. Third, the review will produce a better leader; more able to manage such opportunities in the future - and a better team.

This journey can be a difficult one for the egos that sometimes dominate leaders. Admitting mistakes and omissions can be a difficult challenge for most CEOs. A well-chosen guide can radically improve the return.

In a wonderful article in the November 2004 issue of the Harvard Business Review, Stratford Sherman and Alyssa Freas describe how executive coaches can improve individual and team effectiveness. I would urge every CEO to read that article and pass it around to their senior team.

It is increasingly common that larger organizations, often under the prodding of their Board of Directors, provide their CEOs and 'rising stars' with executive coaches precisely to facilitate the process of leadership growth. From the organizations point of view, providing their key people with mentors makes good sense as it can increase the value of the team member and reduce the chances of a serious, career damaging misstep. From the associates perspective it provides a guide - someone who has 'been there and done that' - has made mistakes and learned - knows the difference between what is good and what is excellent. This investment is increasingly seen as a potent way to increase the value of a team member, the probability that key team members will realize their potentials and the overall effectiveness of the team. It is a win-win-win situation.

I marvel at how infrequently CEOs of emerging companies take advantage of this kind of opportunity - both for themselves and for their key people. Not every CEO is ready for an executive coach. Nor is every team. But those who are should consider the option very carefully. As their company grows, they will have to continually re-invent themselves to meet its needs. As they expand their teams, they need to make sure that they unlock the full potential of each member - and kindle the fires that make each a major factor in the company's growth. As they employ a wider range of strategic advisors, they will have to make sure that the team is getting the most out of the advice received and can turn that advice to the advantage of the company. In all of this there is no substitute for grey hairs and long experience.

Those that know the minefields can run through them - those that don't are casualties waiting to happen.

Chapter 2: Leadership that Limits - The 'Completeness Doctrine'

A while back I was having drinks with a friend who had been involved in coaching senior executives for several decades. During the course of that conversation he offered an interesting and challenging question: *"Why is it that some executives find it so difficult to change behaviors in the face of overwhelming evidence that 1) the behaviors are counterproductive at best and often destructive and 2) that such changes will probably radically improve their effectiveness as a leader - and their contributions to their company?"*

When I asked him what the source of the question was, he recounted a series of coaching situations with much the same (and clearly to him highly frustrating) outcomes. In each case a CEO had, after extended experience with the limiting destructiveness of their own personal tendencies, come up against the distinct possibility that their behavior, rather than the world at large, was the primary source of the factors which were stunting their company's growth.

As he went through the 'case studies', the pattern quickly became clear. Philosophically the question became: *"If humans are capable of rational thought then why doesn't rational thought trump counterproductive behavior in these kinds of situations?"*

I responded initially with one of my favorite aphorisms: *"You can lead a horticulture, but you can't make her think!"* After a good laugh we decided that maybe that was as good a door as any through which to enter this darkened room.

My first foray began with the idea that, for some people, habits, particularly when they relate to important and closely held components of self-image and personality, are very hard to break. My idea was a variation of the old Chinese proverb that once a sheet of paper is folded it will always tend to re-fold in exactly the same place. I suggested that some behavior changes present more of a challenge because they require fundamental modifications in an individual's understanding of who they are. Under the theory that a person's self-image is accumulated over time and plays an essential part not only in defining who that person is to themselves but also what their appropriate place and status in the world is, I suggested that these CEOs were most likely to resist changing behaviors that have come to represent a central part of how they define themselves and how they prefer to be accepted by the world.

This suggestion took us down a path that meandered through a couple of drinks, some tasty, if somewhat overly spicy, hors d'oeuvres and about a half an hour of lively conversation. But the analysis, though logically satisfying, didn't seem to bring us much closer to an answer that might be useful. As satisfying as it was to come to the conclusion that, in some ways and in some situations, people are just mulish, it didn't do much for two people who spend a lot of time and energy trying to help the mule get up and actually pull the wagon.

And, if we were going to attack the problem from that direction both of us should probably take a decade off and get an advanced degree in psychiatry! So I started to look for another possibility.

What was it about these CEOs that seemed to set them apart from others who didn't had the same problems with change? The question seemed daunting. They were a rather incoherent group - managing companies across a range of sizes, industries and value propositions. Some had decades of experience while others were just starting out. There was no apparent dominant gender, age, ethnicity or race trait in the group. So what made them a group? And what caused them to have trouble with achieving fundamental change?

Sometime after the second drink I made a suggestion that seemed to promise a way up. *"Maybe what is important is not the habits that are hard to break but that portion of a person's self-image that tells them they are either still on the journey or that they have arrived."* Maybe this group is a group because all of them subscribe to what I call the "Completeness Doctrine".

I have been fond of observing that *"organizations evolve much more quickly than the people who inhabit them"*. The idea here became *"maybe these people have stopped learning. Perhaps they see themselves as fully formed ... arrived rather than on the journey. Maybe these people have stopped growing!"*

We focused on the personalities of these CEOs and began to dig out some common characteristics. They all had been pretty much rounding the same small circles for years. As another friend is fond of saying, maybe *"they get to confront the same problem over and over until they solve it and then get to go on to the next one."* But, since they aren't capable of solving it, the circular journey continues and the behavior endures.

I left the conversation convinced that we had stumbled on something quite important. Acceptance of the "Completeness Doctrine" as part of an individual's self-image might create limits to growth and change merely through its acceptance. By such an acceptance, an individual might immediately create a whole family of challenges they will not be able to overcome simply because they have closed the books before they developed the necessary skills - they have stopped learning before they have learned what is necessary to know.

On the drive home I remembered people that I had met while on Wall Street who, even well into their 80s, seemed reflexively to take the "student" role when facing the world or new challenges. The combination of wonder and curiosity that they carried with them in all their 'adventures' seemed to re-arrive to my present musings and smile at me over the years - out of a remembrance that had been refreshed.

I have always thought of people who have stopped learning as a kind of 'walking dead'. Their recourse seemed to be to the pettier aspects of life, instrumental interpretations of reality and the delusions that seem to be so necessary to maintain a self-image that awaits only the grave. But now I found myself considering the costs - the terrible costs - that the living are often called upon to pay on account of these 'fossils-of-the-once-alive'.

I'm not sure what the usefulness of these thoughts is - particularly since I have little idea as to how one would go about re-starting the feelings of wonder and curiosity in an individual who has discarded them as distractions. Maybe their only use is a quarantine sign indicating 'no-go' zones for the still living. Maybe the only usefulness of the 'Completeness Doctrine' is as a kind of 'scarlet letter' that should warn investors and potential followers to stay clear of the leper colony.

Or maybe Mary Shelley was right - inorganic matter can be re-enlivened. Now that would be something to see and a cure for many a malaise.

Personally, I am on the side of the monster here. What has been done ill-considered must be capable of being undone with knowledge and will. Otherwise, why bother?

These 'leaders-in-the-swamps-and-mists' must be able to be brought out into the clear air and sunshine. Like all major surgery, it takes the removal of the diseased and the restoration of healthy ways of being.

Chapter 3: A Balanced Senior Management Team

The idea that a senior management team should be balanced is far more easily intellectually accepted than effectively deployed. In my coaching practice, I regularly encounter teams which obviously have been patched together out of 'what was available at the time'. This situation most often is the result of an urgency to get something going and a narrowed vision. But it is important to regularly revisit the question: *"Do I have the right people in the right places to maximize the chances of success?"*

A Balanced Team

The process of designing a balanced team begins with a thoroughgoing assessment of the needs of the company if it is going to thrive in its space. In other words, determining what the team should look like if the company is going to leverage its competitive advantages and beat out its competition. This is a process of determining, given the company's history, resourcing and condition, what would be ideally the right people with the right skills, experiences, and connections in the right slots at the right time.

I believe that this assessment should properly begin with the evolution of a new corporate vision statement and proceed through the development of a substantially revised or completely new strategic plan.

It is at this point that the team leader sometimes objects. "I know my business and what it needs. Why can't I just go out and fill those needs?" Why indeed? In my coaching practice one of the constants has been the weak vision statement that a team leader has for their company. It is, at best, a general and diffused vision and sometimes an ineffective and none-functional one.

A short example might help. Recently one of my clients began the process of developing a new vision statement. His company was growing but more recently slowly than he wanted. Its focus was narrowed on a value proposition that had mostly run its course. Additional progress was possible but growth was going to be limited.

At first the process went slowly … it was difficult for the CEO to see beyond the current focus of his company. We kept at it. Then one morning came the breakthrough … a new vision for the company. We are now in the process of developing a new strategic plan. As a direct result of this process, the definition of what his team needs to be has come into sharp focus and has been expanded. The way ahead is now much clearer.

The Process of Design

Once a vision statement and strategic plan are in place, a comprehensive process is undertaken which is designed to provide the team leader with a framework for making decisions based on an organization's vision statement, strategic plan, mission, budgetary resources, and a set of desired combined team member skill sets.

This process involves an assessment of present team member competencies; an identification of skill sets required; a comparison of the present team strengths and weaknesses with future needs; identification of gaps and excesses; preparation of plans for building the new management team; and a monitoring and evaluation process to assure that objectives are being met.

Effective team development planning requires strong leadership; a clearly articulated vision and mission, and strategic objectives; and by-in by all present members of the management team. It also requires a carefully and realistically designed budgeting process which takes into consideration the resources available to accomplish the mission. This budgeting process needs to allow for the funding for team growth. Once skill sets needed have been defined they must be acquired in a timely fashion. That means that they need to not only be found but also paid for.

The design of the management team is grounded in the needs of the company. A design for a well-balanced and resourced management team provides the existing team with a strategic basis for making team expansion and modification decisions. It allows them to anticipate change rather than being surprised by events or disadvantaged by misalignments.

Some components of the new team will be an expansion of those skill sets presently available within the team. A solid design for team expansion provides more a refined basis for building on existing competencies. Other skill sets will be new to the team. Such a plan will facilitate the integration of those skill sets into the over all management team.

Make no mistake about it; success depends on having the best people with the highest competencies in the right slots and at the right time. Team planning provides a leader with the means of identifying the competencies needed both in the present and also in the future. It provides a reliable guide for developing an effective senior management team.

One more point should be made. Team planning allows a founder to systematically and effectively address issues that are driving change in the company's space. The overall benefits of team planning, then, are to allow the founder to more effectively build a senior management team and improve the chances that that team will succeed in growing the company.

What's In a Plan?

A team development plan should include a management assessment, competency assessments, gap and surpluses analysis, and team evolution planning. The plan should result in a road map which spans the underlying assumptions through to the output of the planning. This establishes the validity of any team development plan by demonstrating the links between team planning and strategic management, budget justifications, the vision statement and mission and both strategic and tactical goals, and human resources planning.

Team development planning provides a leader with a strategic basis for decision-making that is based on achievable goals. Metrics will allow a leader to anticipate turnover (planned or otherwise) and to plan recruiting and team member development ... to move the team toward the team that is needed in the future.

Plans for team transition are inputs to planning for team expansion, internal training, movement, reassignment, and recruiting.

Assessing the Team

A team assessment identifies skill sets, analyzes synergies and identifies gaps and surpluses. A skill set assessment provides baseline data on the existing team. Over time, a trend analysis will provide data on how successfully the team development plan is being implemented. Trend analysis is essential to the effective implementation of any team development plan.

A demand analysis measures future activities and workloads and describes the skill sets needed by the team of the future. Demand analysis must take into account changes in team composition that are driven by changing organizational demands.

Finding the Gaps and Surpluses

A gap analysis compares information from the team assessment and demand analysis. It identifies the differences between the current team competencies and the skill sets needed in the future. The comparison requires that the skill sets defined in the team assessment and the demand analysis phases be comparable ... that is not independently developed. Gap analysis identifies situations in which the number of personnel or competencies in the current team will not meet future needs (demand exceeds supply) and situations in which current competencies exceed the needs of the future (supply exceeds demand).

Planning the Response

This process should result in a response plan for closing gaps in skill sets and reducing surpluses. It will include such things as planned recruiting, training, retraining, and placing or replacing team members. An effective response plan must take into account team member needs or aspirations ... which may work either in favor of or counter to the direction of planned team evolution. The response plan needs to be integrated into the company's strategic plan.

Three components of a well based plan deserve special mention. Management team assessment is a process which defines and quantifies skill sets and competencies (both existing and required to carry out a future function). Conducting a management team assessment requires the leaders of an organization to anticipate how the nature of the organization's focus will change, and then to identify future human resource requirements. A well-based management team assessment is critical to the evolution of an effective plan for team development.

Leadership assessment identifies the attributes that will help each team member become a more effective leader and the behaviors that are limiting both their and the company's growth. Assessing the leadership styles and effectiveness of key team members will help evolve and implement an effective team development plan.

Role analysis describes the conditions of successful job performance. Role analysis focuses on tasks, responsibilities, knowledge and skill requirements as well as other criteria that contribute to successful contributions by each team member. Information collected in this process is used to identify and quantify competencies.

In Summary

Team development planning offers a means of systematically aligning a company's priorities with the budgetary and human resources needed to accomplish them. By beginning the planning process with the development of a new vision statement, revised strategic plan, defined strategic and tactical objectives, leaders can develop a team development plan that will help them accomplish those objectives.

These plans provide a sound basis for justifying budget and team expansion decisions, since there is a clear connection between objectives and the budget and the human resources needed to accomplish them.

To be successful, team development planning requires a solid commitment and leadership from the top. They must lead the planning process, must assure that team development plans are aligned with the vision statement, strategic plan and strategic direction that the company has chosen. They must also hold other team members accountable for carrying out team development planning and implementing the plan. Team members must take responsibility for leading the planning and implementation process.

The results will be a company that will become better aligned with its vision statement, strategic plan and strategic and tactical goals and directions.

Managing Mt. Rushmore

Board meetings are the middle parts of a process which fills the entire calendar year. A company needs to recognize this in order to adequately manage it. In this section I want to talk a bit about the preparation for and management and follow up of the actual meetings. Next I will spend some time on the management of the board between meetings. Finally I will discuss the metrics that are most useful in measuring the progress and contributions of the board.

Goal Number One

The first goal in managing advisory boards as business development engines is to cultivate the emergence and deepening of purposefulness. By that I mean seeing that the culture of the board is focused on obtaining results through the combined purposeful actions of the members and the company's management team.

As its top priority, management needs to help the board members become fully engaged in the future of the company. Initially most board members will be eager to engage but still not integrated into the culture of the company. The board will, at first, be seen as an add-on that the senior team has organized. Both of these situations need to be changed quickly.

Board members need to become 'part of the family'. It is important that they come to feel very deeply connected with the company and its employees. When this happens, they will feel welcomed by the employees and free to communicate with them in a productive and creative way. Management needs to allow this to happen. Any attempts to keep the board as the 'private preserve' of the senior team will limit its effectiveness.

Employees need to see the board as a valuable addition to the company's ability to grow. They have to get to know about the members, their backgrounds, experience and range of contacts as well as their commitment to the company. This is a particularly challenging process as a certain level of formality needs to be maintained. You don't want employees to engage in a lot of ancillary communications with members but you do need to have them supplying important intelligence that will increase the chances of winning new business. Professional courtesy needs to be maintained – particularly with very busy and highly experienced individuals – but it should not get in the way of productivity.

Management needs to put in place a program focused on educating employees about the board – its purpose, function and role. Employees need to know what intelligence to gather and how to pass it up the line. These reporting systems should not be overly engineered. For the most part, I generally recommend that a central clearing point for each member be established within the senior team.

Management should also consider a compensation scheme for employees who gather and pass on important information. Even small rewards such as certificates of recognition are important. For big 'gets' that result in new business gained, cash or options are often a good idea. Incentives should be focused on the provision of meaningful and actionable intelligence.

Remember, purposefulness is the Holy Grail – purposefulness that extends from the senior team through the board – purposefulness that extends down through the ranks. Peak board impact requires a holistic approach to these challenges.

Crisis of Confidence

One area that I focus on as the board gets ready to stand up is the evolution of the relationships between the members and the senior team – particularly the CEO. For most CEOs, dealing with the kind of experienced talent that tends to be assembled can be a challenge to their self-confidence. Behaviors can range from the deferential to avoidance of taking command. Some CEOs simply don't provide the necessary leadership. Others try to micro manage the board. There is a delicate balance that needs to be reached. One of the reasons that I stay involved with the board and its management is to help the senior team – and the CEO in particular - attain this balance.

Early on, we work with the team to help them see the real dynamics that are possible. Members are eager to get to work – to help the company grow. They are going to look to the team for leadership and structure.

"These five people have more total experience than the whole of my senior team. Every one of them has met and mastered challenges that I am still struggling with. How can I presume to lead them? Where do I get off telling Mt. Rushmore to follow me?"

That was how John Slate put it during a conversation we had just before the board was launched. I could see that he was realizing that soon the board would be formed and have its first meeting. *"How do I presume to lead?"* The question seemed to come to him as that time approached.

During the early months of the board's operation, I am heavily engaged in facilitating the development of productive relationships. We work closely with the CEO. In John's case it was a matter of getting him to realize that he had to put those self-doubts away and do the very best he could to provide leadership and structure for the members. He also had to make sure that his senior team was on the same page. We organized a series of training and discussion events and, over the period of a couple of weeks, eased their concerns and got the team focusing on how they would productively participate with board members.

In my early years of building boards, this was one of the challenges that I tended to miss. But now it is one that I focus attention on every time. Management cannot simply assume that they will be able to interact with the members. The board will not allow business as usual. Training in this area prior to launch is one of the most important contributors to a successful launch and purposeful board.

General Observations

A board both generates and lives on high quality intelligence – in both senses of the word. Intelligent management assures that the board can live up to its potential. No matter how motivated and connected members are, poor board management can dissipate enthusiasm and commitment very quickly. The primary burden for making a board work is on the company.

Synergy is a very important aspect of board performance. Effectively gathering, processing and exchange of information are critical to magnifying its impact. Timely and highly useful information is the life blood of any board. Management can set the tone and standards for the gathering and dissemination of this information.

One of the biggest board-killers is the start-then-stop-then-start-then-stop mentality that can settle in if the management team thinks of the board only in terms of its meetings. A board needs to be managed year-round. Members should be engaged year-round. Each time a board stops makes it harder to start it up again. The process generates resistance and pressures. Imagine the cumulative effects of starting then stopping four times a year.

'Event relationships' with board members are the most negative possible outcomes of having a board. If your relationships are centered around the regular meetings and not truly year-round, members will begin to adopt the kind of behavior that I just described. These 'event relationships' become something akin to 'dating' rather than 'living together' and can be tentative in much the same sense. If you are looking to forge a solid connection with these very influential people, you will need to deal with them on an ongoing rather than 'event' basis.

A board thrives on substance and dies when fed fluff. Management needs to make sure that substance is what the board receives. That means forget the 'press release' mentality and the 'chamber of commerce' fluff. You must deliver the kind of actionable intelligence and meaningful tasking that will result in real progress. Board members should not be contacted without purpose and should not be shown off as the 'stars' in the company's heavens. Remember this is a working board – both the management and board members should always have that front and center in their minds.

Board meetings, indeed every contact with any member, should be focused on action and results. Management should reach this understanding early on and be very careful of doing anything to dissipate it. Every meeting should have as its first agenda item a detailed review of progress towards capturing business that has been targeted. Every conversation about a particular piece of business should focus on winning it. Even discussions about new targets - 'brain-storming' discussions of the best ways to pursue these opportunities – should be done with purpose and focus. General discussions which do not conclude with action items and assignment of responsibility for follow-up are corrosive of board performance and should be avoided at all costs.

Remember that the best rule is to 'make heroes and avoid making scapegoats'! Meetings are very good venues in which to single out individuals that have made important contributions. By all means, public recognition is a good idea. It is important to keep that recognition in proportion to the contribution. Board members will realize when a pitch is being over-sold. That being said, other members will take note if the company pauses to recognize the contributions of one of its own.

On the other hand, poor performance should be dealt with privately. Most often these issues come up as a result of a member who is not producing. Many times direct conversations can correct the situation. I have seen members up their game as a result of being treated with consideration. And even if the effort does not improve performance, private discussions will assure that the removal of a member does not cause wider damage.

One question worth consideration is 'who chairs the meetings'? The logical choice might seem the CEO but there are good reasons for taking a more sophisticated approach. I suggest that the agenda be divided into segments and that leadership for each segment be assigned to the person most qualified to lead the discussion. Each time I have used this approach surprising things happen.

Schedule

The board should meet at least four times each year. The major meeting should be coordinated with the annual strategic planning review. Board member participation in this review can be very useful. It will assure that the plan takes into consideration important business opportunities. Involving the board will also strengthen the relationships with management and result in an increased 'buy-in' by members. A broader understanding of the company, its intended direction, resourcing needs and future will also be very helpful.

I have had these meetings productively run on for a couple of days – particularly when important issues such as a liquidity event, strategic partnership formation, major new initiative or significant management change are on the agenda. Sometimes issues will generate contention based on alternative views of the 'best way forward'. In these situations it is always a good idea to allow the process to run its course while the participants are face-to-face. I have always found it a good idea to allow extra time for this most important of all the board meetings.

One approach that I have found very useful is to schedule a presentation of the results of this meeting to either the board of directors or a committee of the outside directors. Both the management team and advisory board members participate in this presentation. The results can be truly galvanizing. Both management and advisors are on the same page – and tied into the same strategic plan.

The meeting that takes place roughly six months after the major one should be focused on progress towards delivering on the strategic plan. It should also allow for a reconsideration of that plan where appropriate. I like to have this meeting face-to-face as well. Compatriots who go more than six months without sitting down and engaging tend to feel less connected.

The other two formally scheduled board meetings can be held via teleconference. These must have the same levels of preparation, materials distribution and structure that the face-to-face ones have. During all of these meetings the reinforcement of the purposefulness needs to be seen to – this is a <u>working board</u> about the serious business of growing the company.

The Materials

Here is a quick set of guidelines for preparing materials prior to a board meeting:

Completeness: Make sure that the package delivered to the members contains all relevant information that they will need to engage on the agenda items. I highly recommend that the package be delivered vie one e-mail or mailing. It is important not to put board members in the position of discussing issues that involve information or documents that they do not have in front of them and/or have not had the time to adequately review. So make sure that they have all the materials that will be used during the meeting. In the event that there are last minute developments, make sure that they are transmitted in a high profile manner and verify that each member has received the update.

Timeliness: If at all possible, deliver the package, including the agenda, at least two weeks prior to the meeting. It is good form to contact each member a few days prior to the session in order to discuss any questions that have come up as a result of their review. This kind of preparation will focus the actual meeting on extending from the information provided rather than focusing on it. Remember that a productive meeting produces progress – from where it started to where it ended up. Timely provision of materials lays the ground for this kind of results.

Professional presentations: This is particularly relevant when it comes to reports of a technical nature such as financials. These reports should follow the professional standards in use by the company. If you ever have spent a frustrating couple of hours trying to reconcile poorly drawn actual performance reports with budget projections you'll know what I mean. Set a high standard for presentations and enforce it.

In usable form: Remember that some of the materials will be useful to members in their contact with potential clients. Get those documents into usable form prior to the meeting. If appropriate, consult with individual members before the session. Don't spend valuable meeting time revising documents!

Between Meetings

The meetings are just the patterns in the rug – there is the woof and warp – the context within which they take place – and that context is a key to broad productivity. Meetings should be a culmination of work done in the 'in-between' times and an opportunity for planning the next steps. The board needs to become a year-round operation. That means that the times between meetings should see the bulk of the activity. This is an important metric and, if not met, an early indicator that something is going astray. A board that becomes active only in the run-up, during the meetings and the period shortly after will atrophy and turn non-productive.

Board members should be regularly updated on intelligence gathered. They should also be contributing information to the mix. *Ad hoc* sessions should be organized when new data indicates either a change in the status of an opportunity being pursued or a new opportunity that has been identified. In such an environment, board members can become valuable sources of high-level intelligence which can, when combined with the more tactical information gathered by employees, radically improve the results of business development efforts.

One particularly potent device is the creation of a special, limited access, virtual bulletin board for both the senior team and the members. It should be a place where new data can be posted with alerts automatically sent out. It should also give members an opportunity to post intelligence that will not be widely accessed.

Measuring the Results

A board is a strategic investment that a company makes with a specific purpose in mind – increasing its growth rate. It should be treated just like any other strategic investment. The board should extend shareholder value by increasing the run-rate, adding to the status of the company in the eyes of potential clients and adding to the value of the company in any liquidation event. As such, investment in a board is properly subjected to the same kind of cost/benefit analysis that other investments are.

What to Measure

The increase in the amount of business in the pipeline is the first metric that you need to pay attention to. This is a very easy one to assess. Most companies keep data on their pipeline. The trend should become more sharply positive within six months of the board's launch.

Another early indicator of board vitality is the amount of time spent by board members in contact with potential clients. Whether in general or targeted conversations, board members should be engaged with important people that will help them identify potential new business. It is important that the senior contact with each member keep a log of conversations on this subject. Not only will these logs become important during planning and review meetings – they will also give an indication of the combined activity of the members on behalf of the company. These levels should deepen and widen over time.

Contact between team and board members is another good indicator of the evolution of productive relationships. It is important that cumulative logs be kept of these contacts and that they are reviewed regularly by the CEO. You will want to look for patterns of both productive and unproductive contact. By reviewing these logs in executive session, a CEO can help his team improve their efforts to get the board operating effectively.

It is important to take the temperature of each member on a fairly regular basis. By that I mean finding out how the member is feeling about their involvement in the board, their role as an advocate for the company and their ability to make significant contributions to its growth. Focus on these issues can help a team identify important areas of work with specific members and support the development of action plans to deal with them. It will also help management detect problems with individual members earlier in their development.

It is important to remember that the time spent by the senior team is an investment in the board. Tracking senior team time should be part of the cost/benefit analysis. This approach will help focus on the productive contacts and reduce their tendency to engage in less productive communications. A system for tracking the time spend should be set up prior to launch of the board.

There are numerous services which track the buzz on a company. By buzz I mean the open source information – positive, negative or neutral – that flows through e-mails, chat rooms and other internet channels. I always recommend that a company arrange for tracking its buzz. It is a very low cost way to find out how a company's reputation is evolving.

Keeping Track of the Pipeline

When assessing the pipeline, there are several factors that need to be taken into consideration. One is the leadership roles by members in identifying, targeting and capturing potential new business. Another is the volume and quality of the leads which each member generates. A third is the lead conversion into proposals. Finally there is the conversion of proposals into won business. Early on the first two factors will be measurable but an indication of the maturing of the board will be that all come into play.

An important metric is the participation of the members beyond the initial, introduction stage. It is vitally important that they stay involved until either the business in won or the effort abandoned. This single indicator will separate out those members who have taken their obligations as advocates very seriously from those who see themselves as providing introductions. An effective member should play an important, ongoing role in any targeting and capture process which result from a lead that they generated.

Collateral Benefits

There are several collateral benefits that accrue to a company that has a board such as the one which I have been describing. Two are worth special mention. First, board members should be regularly bringing senior team members into contact with a wide range of important people. The range and depth of the networks of the team should increase over time. Second, members should be the source of new initiatives – particularly in the business development area. The company should be involved in 'pursuits' that they would not have if the board did not exist.

Reviewing Results

Two things are important about this review process. The first is that the data be provided to all parties – not just the conclusions. The second is that the review be conducted in a completely transparent way for all parties. These to approaches will turn performance review sessions into performance improvement sessions – and that is critical.

It is said that there are two kinds of approaches to managing poor performance. The first is to find someone to blame while the second is to find a way to fix the problem. The first behavior has to be avoided. If reviews become the mechanism to improving performance they will be eagerly anticipated. Management – and the CEO in particular – needs to make this so.

Retrospective

Chapter 1: Anniversary

It had been a year since the launch of the board. It had been through a full series of meetings. But this next meeting was going to be different – it was a strategic review combined with an all-hands retreat.

The year had been a very good one for Rocket Science. Two large pieces of business had been won and board members had been instrumental in helping to win them. One member had been replaced. The working relationships between the team and board members had survived some bumps but were now solid. The reputation of the board within the company had been established – they were a strategic asset.

Everybody in the company had worked hard to win and then deliver on the business. Both contracts were now underway. HR had responded magnificently. They had staffed up two engagements that together amounted to an eighty percent increase in the company's run-rate. Finance had put control systems in place in a highly professional manner. It was a joy to watch people do well what they wouldn't have thought themselves capable of doing at all ten months earlier. Everybody had pitched in and it was time to recognize that.

John decided that a symbolic return to where it all began was just the thing – back to sea and Nassau. So I organized the trip – including a chartered flight for the employees and their traveling companions. We put the group on the very same ship and the senior team and board members in the very same cabins that they had occupied a year before. It was going to be a very nostalgic journey for them.

There were several notable differences between the first and second planning review. The first trip had begun with many uncertainties and had concluded with many questions yet to be answered. The gathering on the pool deck was one of strangers getting to know each other. Some of the sessions were focused on negotiating the rules of engagement and establishing minimum conditions for involvement. Tensions came when the standards of the board members were stricter than those of the management team. It was a time for testing as well as one for deciding if the initial decisions were a good idea.

The return to Nassau was a different experience altogether. The board was obviously working and had proven itself a very good investment. There were no strangers now – only friends who had fought and won battles or were engaged in battles that they expected to win. The rules of engagement had long ago been settled on and the management team had upped its game to meet a much higher set of standards. Now tensions came because of the need to win by working closely together. This was a time for celebrating and for looking forward to a future that was much more clearly defined.

It was also a time to recognize that the board's success had been possible only with the help of everybody within Rocket Science. All of the employees were invited and better than ninety percent of them attended. That amounted to around a hundred fifty employees and a like number of traveling companions. The group was over three hundred and fifty strong!

As a joke I prepared a comparison – how much more a land-based event would have cost the company – and attached a wry suggestion that the savings should be a bonus. John knew that it was a joke – but two weeks after we returned from the trip a rather substantial check showed up. He didn't have to do it – but I remember the gesture and the recognition of the contribution that we had made to him and his company. It is experiences like that that make everything worth while.

The group that assembled on the pool deck was in a serious party mood. They knew that the company was on a path to increased success and they we ready to share the joy that they felt. The evening ended with a private karaoke session. To say 'a good time was had by all' would be an understatement.

John wisely allowed the group to sleep in that first morning at sea. We didn't see most of them until lunch. During the afternoon the employees participated in a series of meetings while the traveling companions enjoyed the ship.

During the first sessions the COO and SVP of business development made presentations. Both referred to their experiences the prior year. Their messages were strongly upbeat. Massive changes had occurred and the company was considerably more professional, better run and growing at an accelerated rate. The COO focused on a cost/ benefit analysis of the board. There was no question – the returns on the modest investment were paying off big time. After Don finished, Linda took the stage. Her presentation outlined the very substantial increase in the reach of the senior team and focused on the massive jump in positive buzz. I could tell that the audience was taking it all in and enjoying every minute of it.

Then John took the stage and introduced each of the board members. He took pains to provide information on the work that each had done and was doing. Each member also made short remarks. They were the stars of his presentation and his gratitude for their support and contributions to the future of the company was evident to all. It was clear they were comfortable being part of the Rocket Science family.

As the afternoon sessions came to a close, John took the stage again. This time he thanked the employees. They had responded magnificently. He singled out several for awards – for their efforts to gather intelligence and assist the board in identifying new business. With that done, he told them that during the next two days they were 'off the clock'. *"Go and enjoy – the thing has been done well and you deserve a break."*

The business part of the trip was over for the employees but the senior team and board members still had work to do. The next morning they began the review of the strategic plan. One thing was different this time – the confidence levels were much higher. Much more seemed possible. The resulting update of the plan was a much more expansive vision for the company and a commitment from each participant to 'make it happen'.

I organized a special dinner in Nassau for the senior team and board members. The ground rules were specific – this was a session to frankly assess and learn from the successes, failures, challenges and advances that the board had experienced during the prior year. Over the years I have found this type of session very important in the maintenance and care of advisory boards.

The discussions were enabled by incredibly good food and lubricated with wonderful wine. Serious failures were frankly discussed without search for blame – only improvement. Successes were celebrated and sealed with toasts all around. Several recommendations were offered by members. The board should be expanded from five to seven with members added in two specific areas. Access to the private bulletin board should be expanded with a special 'reserve area' for very sensitive information. By the time that cigars and brandy showed up, it was clear that this board had an identity that it was comfortable with and a management team that it had confidence in.

With business concluded, the senior team and board settled into a social mode. The final day on the private island was given over to relaxing and enjoying each other's company.

Chapter 2: Assessing the Impact

"Celebrating battles won is fine, but a war won – now there's a cause for celebration!" That is how a friend of mine put it some years ago.

This chapter is about the celebration of a war won. It is now two and a half years after the formation of the board. The mid-way board meeting was held at an all hands summer picnic that the company organized as part of their participation in a local charity fundraising drive. The composition of the board had changed. Three of the original members have left – the one who was asked to resign and two who have 'rooted the pot and retired'. There were also two new seats filled. The board is up to seven members and has a very stable and productive relationship with the senior management team.

We have been through the third strategic plan review. The company is much better at it and this plan is very expansive. We are now half way through the execution on the plan and things are going very well.

Rocket Science is now a much bigger company with a highly professionalized culture and an expanded senior team. Recently they were approached by a strategic buyer. Negotiations are well under way and a liquidity event looks to be a distinct possibility. The board had turned out to be one of the major assets that had attracted the buyer in the first place.

As I sat around a table with the senior team, the conversation turned to how the board had affected each of them. John went first. *"I am a different person because of the board and its members. When I look back at how I used to deal with the role of CEO, I now understand how I was limiting the potential of the company. My role has changed and my understanding of leadership as well. Having these very experienced people as an on-call resource has allowed me to grow in ways I never anticipated. Letting Chief build the board was one of the best decisions I've ever made."*

Don went next. *"I can't believe how much my role as COO of the company has changed over time. In one way I am dealing with a much narrower remit. Lots of things that were once on my plate, Lois now sees to. In another way, I am much busier than I was back then. And I spend much more time supervising others than doing the actual work."*

Linda talked about the effect that the board had on her understanding of business development. *"Before the board I saw the process as one of knocking on doors and trying to get a foot in. I was determined to make the old model work. I have kept the cards of every middle-level person that we had in the slots and last week I looked at all of them. I am amazed at the money we spent on what turned out to be a series of dead ends. Now I have a process that I am sure works. All those business cards are just reminders of what used to be and should be no more."*

There is no payment of any kind that can compare with helping people accomplish what they only dreamt of. The satisfaction of that time was overwhelming. These good people had met and overcome their limitations and had discovered themselves and each other in the process.

Whatever challenges came, they were ready for them. Whatever opportunities came before them, they were up to taking advantage of them. But most importantly, whoever they were capable of becoming, they were ready to become.

Final Thoughts

After reading the chapters I am concerned that a reader might get the impression that designing, standing up and managing an advisory board that drives corporate growth is either an easy or straightforward exercise. Before closing I want to disabuse anyone that has come to that conclusion.

This much is true. My advisory boards are the single most effective way to drive a company's top line that I have ever found. Correctly done, the process can truly generate an amazing pace. There is no question in my mind that the presence of five to seven highly experienced, well connected and committed senior individuals has a far greater impact on the future of a company than any other resourcing.

I have watched management teams struggle with the need to up their game in anticipation of launching a board. Some have backed off of the challenge – realizing that the road is either too difficult or leads in a direction that, after reflection, they don't want to travel.

I have also helped teams come to the conclusion that, although they do want to travel those pathways, they need to take some time to prepare themselves and their company for the journey. This honorable and courageous decision has saved many from wasting precious resources and substantial negative branding.

Some management teams have tried and failed. Whether through a lack of will or potential, they were forced to the conclusion that they were not up to the challenge.

But, most often, teams have faced their limitations and overcome them. They have mastered the need to reinvent themselves in order to better serve the needs of their company and compatriots. And it is these experiences that make the effort so worthwhile.

The challenge is to make business development live up to its name – to master the single most ubiquitous point of pain that any management team faces and turn it into an advantage that will allow a company to beat out its competition and become master of its future. An advisory board is the best way to do precisely that.

Contact Information

I sincerely hope that you have enjoyed this book and find it useful. I am always interested to hear from readers – about their thoughts on the book or relevant war stories that relate to it. Please feel free to send either to DrSmith@Dr-Smith.com.

If you are interested in exploring the possibility of an advisory board for your company, send me an e-mail. Provide us with as much information as you can. We will contact you to arrange a free consultation.

You can learn more about me by visiting my website: http://.wwwDr-Smith.com

www.ingramcontent.com/pod-product-compliance
Lightning Source LLC
Chambersburg PA
CBHW051535170526
45165CB00002B/746